THE
GEORGIANS
IN 100
FACTS

MIKE RENDELL

AMBERLEY

Dedicated to my ever-patient wife Philippa, who has to cope with my prolonged absences in the eighteenth century.

First published 2015

Amberley Publishing
The Hill, Stroud
Gloucestershire, GL5 4EP

www.amberley-books.com

British Library Cataloguing in Publication Data.
A catalogue record for this book is available from the British Library.

ISBN 978 1 4456 4780 7 (paperback)
ISBN 978 1 4456 4781 4 (ebook)

Typeset in 11pt on 13.5pt Sabon.
Typesetting and Origination by Amberley Publishing.
Printed in the UK.

The Facts

Introduction   7
1. George I Elevated Both the Maypole and the Elephant to the Peerage   8
2. Each King George Fell Out with His Son, Big Time   9
3. 1715 Was 'Mar'd' by Rebellion   11
4. The South Sea Bubble Led to Guy's Hospital, but Newton Lost a Mint   12
5. Jenkins Lost an Ear and All Hell Broke Loose in Parliament   14
6. Reading the Riot Act Really Did Happen after 1715   16
7. The Grand Tour Brought Italy to Our Doorstep   17
8. Gin Was Sold by the Barrow – and Drunk by the Pint   19
9. The People Who Worked on Beaver Pelts Really Did Become 'as Mad as a Hatter'   20
10. William Kent Was Considered to Be a Better Garden Designer than Architect   21
11. The Georgians Just Loved Joining Clubs   22
12. A Vicar Discovered Aspirin 2,000 Years after the Greeks Forgot It   24
13. Men Were Peacocks – from Macaronis to Dandies and Exquisites   26
14. The Georgians Drank an Awful Lot of Hot Drinks   27
15. Handel Gave Us *Zadok*, *Water Music* and *Messiah*   28
16. *The Beggar's Opera* Made John Rich Gay and John Gay Rich   29
17. The Waters of Bath May Have Tasted Foul, but There Were Thousands of Takers   31
18. Mr Bramah Not Only Invented the Flush Toilet but a Lock to Go with It   32
19. Mr Addis Made Both a Toothbrush and a Fortune   33
20. Commodore Anson Hijacked a Ship and Brought Home a Fortune   35
21. If the Pox Didn't Kill You, the Cure Definitely Would   36
22. The '45 Rebellion Caused the Nine of Diamonds to Be Known as 'the Curse of Scotland'   38
23. The '45 Rebellion Led to the Ordnance Survey   40
24. The '45 Rebellion Also Helped Improve Our Roads   41
25. At 282 Days, 1751 Was the Shortest Year on Record   42

26. The Seven Years War Didn't Last Seven Years 44
27. Clive Was Amazed at His Own Moderation 46
28. The State Lottery Existed Long Before Camelot 48
29. The Lunar Society Had Lunarticks as Members 50
30. Print Shops Helped Turn the Famous into Celebrities 52
31. Cosmetics Were to Die For 54
32. John Wesley Agreed to Disagree 56
33. James Cook Never Lived to Enjoy Valentine's Day 58
34. Coal Was King When George Was on the Throne 60
35. The East India Company Was a Superpower in Its
    Own Right 62
36. Laudanum Addicts Gave Way to Cokeheads 64
37. George III May Not Have Been Mad to Start with,
    but He Was by the End 66
38. The Chippendales Were Considered Wooden, but
    Polished 68
39. One Man Can Claim to Have Been the Father of
    Civil Engineering 70
40. Josiah Wedgwood Was Definitely Not Potty 72
41. Sir Joshua Reynolds Loved Painting Whores 74
42. 'Snuffy Charlotte' Helped Promote Brightly
    Coloured Hankies 76
43. Banknotes Were a Licence to Print Money 78
44. Bristol Blue Was Not West Country Pornography 80
45. With William Pitt It Really Was a Case of 'Like
    Father, Like Son' 82
46. Charles Fox Was a Politician Who Gambled, Lost a
    Fortune, but Won Love 84
47. If Priestley Had His Way We Would All Be Breathing
    Dephlogisticated Air 86
48. The Poor Prayed 'Give Us Our Daily Bread' – but
    Many Went Without 88
49. Excessive Sugar Consumption Gave Dentists a Busy Time 90
50. Modern Horse Racing Traditions Started with the
    Georgians 92
51. Shoelaces Made Metal Workers Redundant 94
52. Manufacturers of Tinder Boxes and Flintlocks Hated
    Mr Walker 96
53. To Be Frank, It Was Never an Entire Necessity to
    Have an Envelope 98

54. 'Capability' Brown Destroyed More Gardens than Anyone Else Before or Since   100

55. 'Get Off My Land!' – the Enclosure Acts Drove the Rural Poor into Towns   102

56. Not All of His Inventions Involved Hot Air – James Watt Also Invented a Portable Copier   104

57. Paul May Have Been Revered by One George (Washington) but Never by Another (George III)   106

58. Mr Churchman Made Exceedingly Good Chocolate   108

59. Australia Was Never a Holiday Destination   110

60. Smugglers Loved War with France   112

61. Counterfeiting Coins Was Deadly   114

62. Global Cooling, Not Warming, Was a Hot Topic   116

63. Jethro Tull Never Played the Flute   118

64. Jane Austen Remained Anonymous Throughout Her Lifetime   120

65. Ketchup Was Never Red   122

66. Philip Astley Never Ran Away to Join the Circus   124

67. One Man Links Both 'Rule Britannia!' and 'God Save the King!'   126

68. Carlton House Was a Palace Fit for a Prince, but Not for a King   128

69. Pope Joan Was Extremely Popular   130

70. The Prince of Wales Caused a Tartan Mania   132

71. Bridges Didn't Last Forever   134

72. There Were Various Attempts to Assassinate George III   136

73. James Cox Had a Museum That Everyone Wanted to See   138

74. One Man Doubled the Size of the Solar System   140

75. Everyone Looked to the Skies in 1784 – and Many Had Their Pockets Picked   142

76. Everyone Had Their Favourite Hobby in 1819   144

77. Dr Johnson Had the Last Word in Lexicography   146

78. Matthew Boulton Made a Mint – the Royal Mint   148

79. Buckingham Palace Was the Queen's House   150

80. Mary Wollstonecraft Was the Mother of Frankenstein   151

81. Hannah More Showed That Women Counted – and Could Read Too, If Schooled   153

82. Admission to Almack's Was the True Mark of Social Status   155

83. The Lord Mayor's Carriage Has Not Needed an MOT or a Road Licence in 250 Years — 157

84. Merlin Invented the Roller Skate, but Not the Brake for It — 159

85. Thomas Clarkson Was the True Father of Abolition — 161

86. All That Glittered Was Not Necessarily Gold, or Silver — 163

87. A Small Fishing Village Called Brighthelmstone Became Fashionable Brighton — 165

88. It Was No Fun Being an Animal — 167

89. There Were Two Brunels, and One of Them Was Georgian — 169

90. Edward Jenner, Smallpox Pioneer, Was an Authority on the Cuckoo — 171

91. Nelson Was a Legend in His Own Lifetime — 173

92. Nelson Wanted the Nation to Look After Emma, but after Trafalgar, It Didn't — 175

93. War with France Meant Income Tax and High Inflation — 177

94. Napoleonic War Medals Were Awarded Rather Late — 179

95. Gas Lighting Enabled Factory Staff to Work Shifts — 181

96. You Couldn't Have Had an Industrial Revolution Without Mr Maudslay's Nuts and Bolts to Hold It Together — 183

97. The Queen Was Barred at Bayonet Point from Entering the Abbey — 185

98. Only the Rich Got Divorced — 187

99. Dr Buchan's Work Meant That Anyone Could Recognise a Buboe — 189

100. We Nearly Had Queen Charlotte and Not Queen Victoria — 191

Introduction

The 300th anniversary of the accession of George I to the throne of Great Britain has led to a renewal of interest in the Hanoverians, with countless books, radio and TV programmes, films and exhibitions. So, why another book? Because this is for grazers – people who wish to dip in and out of the period, who like their history in bite-sized chunks rather than in large doses.

The Georgian era was an extraordinary time – the start of the British Empire, the loss of the American colonies and the birth of what became the Industrial Revolution. Above all, it was a time when a small number of men and women stood head and shoulders above their contemporaries – people who changed their world, and ours, by their vision, their determination and their genius.

1. George I Elevated Both the Maypole and the Elephant to the Peerage

George I had a disastrous relationship with his wife: he thought it was fine for him to have mistresses, but took an extremely dim view of his wife's infidelities. His wife was actually his cousin Sophia and, having borne her husband two children, she embarked on an affair with a Swedish count. He was murdered, and the royal marriage was dissolved. Sophia spent the rest of her life – thirty years – in exile, forbidden to see her children.

When George arrived in England in 1714, his claim to the British throne was based on the fact that the fifty other claimants were either Catholic or had Catholic sympathies. George was a Protestant, albeit a rather charmless, adulterous and allegedly incestuous one. He was never popular with his subjects, and he showed little fondness for the country, its language or its customs.

The allegations of incest arose because it was widely assumed that one of the two women who accompanied him to England as his mistress was his half-sibling. She was another Sophia, but was nicknamed 'the Elephant', and was the daughter of one of his father's mistresses. Nobody could be sure who her father was. The king's other mistress, Melusine, was known as 'the Maypole', and was a scrawny, willowy figure. Neither the Elephant nor the Maypole were popular figures, but each in turn was rewarded for her loyalty by being elevated to the peerage – Melusine as the Duchess of Kendal, and Sophia as the Countess of Leinster.

2. Each King George Fell Out with His Son, Big Time

The man who succeeded George I as king was his son, who became George II in 1727. Given that he had been taken from his mother's side when he was ten, and was forbidden leave to visit her throughout her exile, it is not surprising that he was continually at loggerheads with his father. George I would not allow his son to join the army, at least not until the prince had produced a male heir, but once young George and his new wife were married and had children, other difficulties arose. A public disagreement at the christening of their second child led to the royal couple being banished from Court, and, for a time, being barred access to their young family. The couple set up a new London residence, known as Leicester House, and this quickly became a meeting place for the opponents of the king. In consequence of his son's unsuitable friendships, King George declined to appoint him regent during the king's frequent visits to Hanover. It was during one of these visits that George I died. His son refused to go to Hanover for the funeral, thereby endearing himself considerably to the British public.

George II had just as bad a relationship with his own son, Frederick, Prince of Wales, which was hardly surprising given that Frederick was left behind in Hanover when the family decamped to England in 1714, and he didn't see them again for fourteen years. He came to England as a young man, a year after his father became king, and by then was already exhibiting a fondness for drinking, gambling and womanising. Father and son were strangers and did not get on. As Prince of Wales, Frederick was always short of money, but when he applied to Parliament for an increased allowance, his father opposed the idea.

Frederick developed a rival court at Leicester House, which became a hotbed of opposition, attracting all those who were disgruntled by the activities of Walpole's government. When the wife of the prince was due to give birth, Frederick drove the expectant mother through the night from Windsor to central London. He was desperate to keep the baby, once born, out of the king's clutches. George II was furious and banished his son from Court. When the Prince of Wales died suddenly at the age of forty-four, in 1751, his eldest son, Prince George, became heir apparent, finally acceding to his grandfather's throne as George III in 1760.

The new king was a prolific breeder – he had fifteen children, but was perpetually at war with his eldest child, George, Prince of Wales. George III was opposed to anything extravagant or ostentatious, whereas the prince was always happiest whoring, gambling and drinking. For the prince, excess was never enough. George III also distrusted his son because of the way he was aligned to the radical opposition party, led by Charles Fox. Small wonder the two men were implacable opponents.

Years later, when it was the turn of George, Prince of Wales, to be a parent, he continued with the Hanoverian tradition of being an overbearing but often absent father. Parenting skills were definitely not a Hanoverian forté!

3. 1715 WAS 'MAR'D' BY REBELLION

By the time James Francis Edward Stuart landed in Scotland from France, just before Christmas in 1715, his 'popular uprising' was already doomed to failure: he stayed in the country just six weeks – long enough for a quick coronation and a spot of sightseeing – before leaving Scotland forever. The rebellion against the Hanoverian monarchy was supported by many Scots, particularly in the central highlands. John Erskine, Earl of Mar, had raised the royal standard of 'James VII of Scotland and James III of England' in September 1715. His forces captured Inverness, Aberdeen and Dundee, before clashing with government forces led by the Duke of Argyll, at Sheriffmuir. Despite outnumbering the enemy by three to one, Mar failed to press home a somewhat indecisive victory, fell back and allowed Argyll's troops to regroup.

The problem for the Old Pretender (as the would-be James III was known) was not just that Mar lacked leadership and direction; the uprising failed to gain favour south of the border. Expecting trouble, the government had already moved troops into the south-west of England, effectively stifling opposition from an area where Jacobite support was thought to be high. There was, however, a small uprising in Northumberland, where the rebels combined with a force of Scottish Borderers and headed south. They got as far as Preston, Lancashire, before battle with the English was joined. After two days of bitter fighting the government forces prevailed. The rebels put down their weapons and either surrendered or, like Mar, went into exile in France.

4. The South Sea Bubble Led to Guy's Hospital, but Newton Lost a Mint

When the South Sea Bubble burst in 1720 it sent shock waves across the nation: fortunes were lost overnight, especially among the emerging middle class. They were the merchants and businessmen who had ploughed their profits back into a scheme which, for nine years, had seemed to be a sure-fire winner. When the country's first major stock market crash came, it came with a vengeance.

The South Sea Company had started off as a joint-stock venture to capitalise on trade with South America. In practice, such trade was wholly in the hands of the Spanish, but the stock rose on the basis that it was hoped that the monopoly would be broken. The scheme was also an umbrella organisation for a host of scams – ingenious bits of flimflam with no hope of profit, but dressed up with hype and falsehood. There was, for instance, a plan 'for making money, but no one to know what it is' and a raft of other spurious plans which sounded good, but which had no financial justification whatsoever. Ideas for extracting sunshine from vegetables, or developing perpetual motion machines, should never have fooled anyone with any common sense, but that was a commodity in short supply with the frenzied mob of punters eager to get rich quick.

A scheme was cooked up whereby the company would consolidate the national debt. Insider trading ensured huge profits for the directors when the stock rose dramatically once the scheme became public. Enormous bribes were given to politicians and to influential people in order to ensure that the scheme got off the ground without too many awkward questions being asked in Parliament. For years the stock had doubled and re-doubled, and many persons of rank and wealth took out loans or pledged their land as security for stock purchases. The ostensible gains were huge: stock which had stood at £128 in January 1720, rose to £175 in February, £330 in March and £550 at the end of May. At its peak in August, shares were trading at £1500, but within a month the crash had brought the value down to one-tenth of that figure. Even Sir Isaac Newton, Master of the Royal Mint at the time, lost out. When the crash came, he burnt his fingers to the tune of £30,000 – equivalent to perhaps £2.5 million today. Many people were forced into bankruptcy, and the crash caused real damage to the national economy. Robert Walpole and his ministry had to clear up the mess, which he did with considerable skill, but not without infuriating many who saw him as part of the central problem of corruption and greed. Many of the perpetrators of the fraud fled abroad.

Some people did get out in time: Sir Thomas Guy was fortunate enough to sell before the crash, with profits of £50,000 – more than enough to endow a fine hospital which still bears his name today.

5. Jenkins Lost an Ear and All Hell Broke Loose in Parliament

When the brig *Rebecca*, commanded by Captain Robert Jenkins, was boarded off the coast of Florida by Spanish coastguards in 1731, Jenkins was roughed up to the extent that his ear was sliced off. Little would the aggrieved owner of the ear have thought that nearly 130 years later the writer Thomas Carlyle would use the ear, and the Jenkins name, to describe a war with Spain which started in 1739 and lasted until 1748. Until 1742 it was a purely Britain versus Spain spat, aimed at dissuading the Spanish from reneging on a deal whereby the British were permitted to trade with the Spanish colonies.

The trade agreement was known as the *asiento*, and gave Britain limited trading rights with the Spanish territories in the New World. 500 tonnes of goods could be sold each year. For years Britain had stretched the rules to the limit. Technically only one ship a year was allowed to trade, but in practice that one ship was replenished by numerous other vessels lying out of sight, further offshore. The trade was highly profitable, and the British were worried that Spain would try and cancel the trading privilege. Parliament saw the assault on Captain Jenkins as an indication that the Spanish thought that the British could be pushed around. Much jingoistic hot air filled the House of Commons, and Captain Jenkins was called before Parliament to give evidence.

In his original deposition, Jenkins had stated that the Spanish captain had tied him to the mast and sliced off his ear with a cutlass. Jenkins also alleged that the Spanish captain said that he was to go back and tell

George II that the same would happen to the king if he was ever caught by the Spanish.

As a final push for war, a jar was produced in the House, apparently containing the pickled remains of the missing ear. It was enough to outrage Parliament – how *dare* a Spaniard do such a thing to an English master mariner? – regardless of the fact that the British had been doing the same (and far, far worse) to the Spanish for many years. War against Spain was declared in 1739, giving rise to Walpole's famous comment, 'They are ringing their bells, soon they will be wringing their hands.'

The War of Jenkins' Ear mostly involved actions in the West Indies, Panama and various parts of coastal South America. The conflict involved much privateering (government-approved piracy) by both Spanish and English ships.

By 1742 the spat with Spain became part of the larger conflict known as the War of Austrian Succession. This centred on the rival claims of Prussia and Austria to the lands known as Silesia, and brought the emphasis of the fighting back from the Caribbean and South America, onto mainland Europe. The war dragged in most of the European powers, with France entering the fray in 1744. It continued until the 1748 Treaty of Aix-La-Chapelle.

6. READING THE RIOT ACT REALLY DID HAPPEN AFTER 1715

When George I came to the throne there was rioting in several cities across the country, and there was a very real fear that there would be support for a Jacobite attempt to reclaim the throne. Parliament wanted local authorities to have the power to deal firmly with rioters, without fear of being blamed after the event if there was collateral damage to innocent passers-by or property. The Riot Act came into force on 1 August 1715. It provided that the mayor, sheriff or JP could 'read the Riot Act' and, in doing so, order the dispersal of any group of more than twelve people who were 'unlawfully, riotously, and tumultuously assembled together'. Failure to disperse within one hour was a felony punishable by death.

To be valid, the reading of the Riot Act had to be word-perfect, and the courts refused to recognise the validity if any of the prescribed words were omitted – even the ending, 'God save the King.'

The Act was invoked on two particular occasions – in 1768 before the Massacre of St George's Fields, and at the Peterloo Massacre in 1819. In the first case, an unlawful assembly started to protest against the imprisonment of John Wilkes (author of an article in the *North Briton*, severely criticising George III). Troops opened fire, killing half a dozen people. At Peterloo, some 70,000 people gathered in Manchester to demand the reform of parliamentary representation. The Act was read, and troops opened fire, killing sixteen people and injuring hundreds more.

7. The Grand Tour Brought Italy to Our Doorstep

Any well-to-do aristocrat would expect to spend his early twenties on the Grand Tour, a sort of rite of passage for the young. As the historian Edward Gibbon wrote, 'According to the law of custom, and perhaps of reason, foreign travel completes the education of an English gentleman.'

Having gone to Oxford or Cambridge, the young gentleman would follow a well-trodden path through France, before entering Italy via Switzerland and going to Turin, Florence, Venice, Rome and perhaps Naples. The newly discovered remains at Pompeii and Herculaneum were also on many agendas. For some, the Grand Tour took a matter of months. For others, it lasted years. James Caulfeild, 1st Earl of Charlemont, was gone fully nine years before he bothered to come home.

The tour really came into its own during the Georgian era, bringing the cream of the country's wealthy young men into contact with continental, and especially Italian, influences. They brought these influences back, and when designing and furnishing their new country homes, they looked no further than what they had already seen on their continental tours. In came Palladian architecture, classical colonnades and niches filled with statues in the Roman style. The young nobles returned from their tour with their language skills suitably honed, and with their luggage full of portable antiques such as medallions, coins and ornaments in the classical style. These then filled the display cabinets back home, even if the 'antiquities' were only made a few months earlier in a backstreet workshop. It all helped to establish a love of all things Italian. Paintings were influenced by Classical and Renaissance styles, with putti (cherub-like small boys) seemingly floating above every Baroque masterpiece. Italian opera, sung by Italian castrati and sopranos, filled our opera houses.

Accompanying the young gentleman would have been a guide-come-tutor-come-chaperone known as a bear-leader, a man who had the job of making sure that all the right things were seen and appreciated. The travelling group might also include a cook and a number of servants. Along the way the party might well join forces with other similar groups, or rub shoulders with young artists and sculptors sent to Italy from England in order to develop their skills and to copy Italian works of art. Artists such as Joshua Reynolds and William Kent both polished their skills in this way.

In time, the tour went downmarket, and by the Victorian era it was conducted by train – and even included women. It became a package holiday for the aspirational and lost its aristocratic credentials. However, in its heyday it was a wonderful way of allowing young noblemen the chance to sow their wild oats, away from parental control, while mixing with people of their own class and forming bonds of friendship which lasted a lifetime. Besides, a little bit of culture never did anyone any harm, although in the case of some of the Grand Tourists, it probably didn't do much good either.

8. Gin Was Sold by the Barrow – and Drunk by the Pint

The Gin Craze lasted throughout the first half of the eighteenth century. Gin was a popular Dutch drink introduced to this country after the Glorious Revolution in 1688. When war with France led to shortages of brandy, the drinking public turned to gin with a vengeance. This was helped when the distilling monopoly enjoyed by the London Guild of Distillers was broken in 1690.

Gin became cheap, hence the slogan, 'Drunk for a penny; dead drunk for twopence.' It was a ferociously strong drink, at 160° proof. Illegal distilleries were known to flavour the tipple not with juniper berries, but with highly poisonous substances such as turpentine and sulphuric acid.

London's poor, faced with grinding poverty, knocked it back by the tankard. It meant a veritable epidemic of drunkenness, causing a significant spike in mortality rates and leading to all manner of social evils. Prostitution and violence increased. Parliament sought to eradicate the problem, passing five different Gin Acts over a twenty-two-year period. The 1736 Gin Act introduced a licensing system whereby distillers were to pay an astronomic fee of £50 a year. It drove production underground, and only two licences were ever granted. In 1751 a new Act was passed, reducing the annual licence fee. It also outlawed the sale of gin in barrows and stalls by only permitting sales from premises where the rent exceeded £10 per annum. The epidemic came to an end when food prices rose. Farmers sold their grain to millers for bread, rather than to the distilleries for gin.

9. THE PEOPLE WHO WORKED ON BEAVER PELTS REALLY DID BECOME 'AS MAD AS A HATTER'

To be 'as mad as a hatter' was a term used to describe dementia in hat-factory workers, caused by working with mercury. Daily exposure to mercury also led to problems with vision, hearing and speech, along with coordination difficulties.

For over 200 years the beaver had been hunted throughout North America, almost to the point of extinction. The beaver brought enormous profits to the Hudson Bay Company, which was founded in 1670 and flourished throughout the 1700s. The success of the company played an important part in the opening up of Canada, by bringing increasing numbers of trappers to the province. Conditions were harsh, because the best beaver pelts were from animals captured in the winter.

The beaver has two types of hair: a coarse outer guard hair and a soft under layer, called beaver wool. The pelts would be brought back to London, where mercuric salts dissolved in nitric acid were applied in a procedure known as carrotting, so that the beaver wool could be pulled out.

Once the beaver wool had been agitated, pummelled and boiled to produce a thick felt, it could be shaped into different styles on a hat-making block. This involved using steam, but the process had the unfortunate effect of releasing the toxic mercury fumes, inhaled constantly by the workers.

By the early 1800s hats produced from felted beaver fur were going out of fashion, to be replaced by top hats made from silk 'hatter's plush'.

10. William Kent Was Considered to Be a Better Garden Designer than Architect

William Kent was a painter, an architect and a garden designer; a man you either loved or hated. Hogarth, for one, held him in low esteem, dismissing him as a 'contemptible dauber'.

He spent ten years in Rome, meeting and greeting young lords on the Grand Tour, and acting as a procurer of paintings and antiquities. He befriended a lot of the wealthy movers and shakers of the time. Richard Boyle, Lord Burlington, encouraged Kent to give up painting and take up architecture. Having edited a book on the designs of Inigo Jones, Kent developed a revised Palladian style and used it at Holkham Hall for Thomas Coke, 1st Earl of Leicester. Royal support resulted in him being appointed master carpenter to the Office of Works. His designs for the Treasury building and the Horse Guards building, both in Whitehall, demonstrate his importance and influence. Prince Frederick also gave him the title of Architect to the Prince of Wales. In return, Kent designed a splendid royal barge for the prince, which has pride of place at the National Maritime Museum.

As a landscape gardener he paved the way for the open, park-like settings favoured by later exponents such as Capability Brown, and his designs can still be seen at Stowe and at Rousham House. For him, a garden meant grassy knolls, dotted with classical temples. His remark that 'all gardening is landscape painting' continues to influence garden designers today. Kent also designed furniture and interiors, including those at Chiswick House.

11. The Georgians Just Loved Joining Clubs

One of the features of the Georgian era was the fascination with joining clubs and societies. There was a great range of associations where like-minded people could meet. 1717 saw four of London's medieval Freemasonry Lodges come together as a Grand Lodge, meeting at the Goose and Gridiron tavern in St Paul's Churchyard. An Irish Grand Lodge started in 1725 and a Scottish one in 1736, and from there freemasonry spread throughout the British colonies.

Other groups included the Hellfire Club, first founded in 1718. It reappeared in 1746 as Sir Francis Dashwood's Order of the Friars of St Francis of Wycombe – a curious assembly of rakes and 'persons of quality' who met at the George and Vulture. From there it moved to Medmenham Abbey, where members indulged in pagan rites and much drinking and fornication. Whores, known colloquially as 'nuns', were brought in for the entertainment of the participants.

The Sublime Society of Beef Steaks was established in 1735 by theatre manager John Rich, and attracted members from the theatre, the arts and the military. The Prince of Wales joined in 1785, and would have taken part in the weekly meetings where steaks and potatoes were consumed. Members included John Wilkes, William Hogarth, Samuel Johnson and (probably) David Garrick, so it is fair to assume that the luncheon would have been followed by much revelry, with witticisms and good conversation flowing with the wine.

The excesses of the Hellfire Club led to a resurrection

of the Society for the Reformation of Manners in the 1750s. It had first started in the 1690s and had been active in the early years of George I in bringing prosecutions against the owners of brothels and molly houses (where homosexuals held their meetings). Later, its activities were subsumed in the Society for the Suppression of Vice set up by William Wilberforce in 1787.

Not all the clubs were limited to men: the Blue Stockings Society was a literary discussion group formed in the 1750s. Men were allowed to attend as guests, and the society was a ground-breaker in that it encouraged women to take part in intellectual discussions, with an emphasis on education and learning.

Other groupings arose out of the earlier coffee houses, with both Boodles and Brooks's being formed in 1762. They were gambling houses for the extremely rich and well-connected, with Brooks's being associated with the Whigs. The older White's became the unofficial headquarters of the Tory party in 1783, and it was here, in a specially constructed bow window, that Beau Brummell would survey the passing scene and pronounce on matters of dress and style.

Some clubs developed because of sporting connections. Thomas Lord raised money to buy land where cricket was played to rules laid down by the Marylebone Cricket Club, founded in 1787. Throughout the country, men (and, to a lesser extent, women) rushed to join societies and clubs where they could meet like-minded people and develop hobbies and interests.

12. A Vicar Discovered Aspirin 2,000 Years after the Greeks Forgot It

Next time you reach for a bottle of aspirin to treat your headache, back pain or rheumatic fever, spare a thought for good old Edward Stone, a vicar who lived at Chipping Norton in Gloucestershire. One day, in around 1757, he was walking across the meadow near his home. Willow trees were thriving in the damp, boggy conditions and he idly stripped off a piece of the willow bark (as one does) and chewed it. Now, willow bark is extremely bitter, and the good Reverend immediately remembered another very bitter bark – one brought back from South America and known at the time as 'Jesuit's powder' or 'Peruvian bark'. Unbeknown to the apothecaries who prescribed it for its beneficial qualities, the bark contained quinine.

Stone cleverly surmised that the bitter willow might have similar beneficial qualities to Jesuit's powder. He carried out an experiment by gathering a pound of common white willow bark. He dried it by hanging it in a bag over a bread-oven for three months, and then pulverised it with a pestle and mortar to create a dry powder. He split it up into small doses and administered it to around fifty ague-ridden parishioners (amazing to think how many gullible people must have been living in Chipping Norton at the time – 'Trust me, I'm a vicar, now swallow this bitter pill'). Every one of the victims/patients noticed an improvement, or as the vicar himself said, the pills 'were a powerful astringent and very efficacious in curing agues and intermittent disorders.'

Stone conducted a series of clinical trials to ascertain the most effective dose. As he was later to write,

> Being an entire stranger to its nature I gave it in very
> small quantities, I think it was about twenty grains of
> the powder at a dose, and repeated it every four hours
> ... Not perceiving the least ill consequences I grew
> bolder with it and in a few days increased the dose to
> two scruples, and the ague was soon removed.

He administered the powder 'with any common vehicle such as tea, water or small beer' and noted the time taken for the patient to improve. In fact he had discovered salicylic acid, the active ingredient in aspirin. On 25 April 1763, he wrote a letter to Lord Macclesfield, the President of the Royal Society, outlining his researches of the previous six years and giving details of the findings. They were published shortly afterwards.

Ironically, the painkilling qualities of willow bark had been known to the ancient Greeks – Pliny and Hippocrates had both extolled its virtues some 2,000 years earlier – but the knowledge had since disappeared. Stone's scientific approach kick-started more research; not bad going for a vicar with no medical or scientific training. 'Aspirin' was the brand name given to the compound some ninety years later. Stone's achievement is marked with a blue plaque, erected near his old house in Chipping Norton.

13. Men Were Peacocks – from Macaronis to Dandies and Exquisites

One spectacular consequence of the Grand Tour was that its participants came back with a liking for Italian fashion. Men adopted a style of dressing quite foreign to the Englishman who had stayed at home, and who now stood watching in amazement as men strutted their stuff in ever-taller wigs, twirling their walking canes and peering at the world through quizzing glasses. These preposterous poodles became known as 'macaronis' – a term which emanated from the fact that, like pasta, the fashion originally came from Italy. In time their fashions were copied by others who had never set foot outside the country, presumably as a pretence that they too had been on an Italian adventure. The song 'Yankee Doodle Dandy' ridicules this affectation, with the line, 'Stuck a feather in his hat and called it macaroni.'

The ostentatious behaviour was not confined to fashion: macaronis were renowned for speaking in an affected silly style and for their effeminate manners. As such they were a world apart from the rather later dandies (otherwise known as beaus, exquisites or gallants). The dandy was not originally an effeminate creature; he was an immaculately dressed person who adopted the nonchalant airs and graces of the aristocracy, and who somewhat slavishly followed the dictates of men like Beau Brummell. George Bryan Brummell, to give him his full name, was born in 1778 and became a friend of the Prince Regent, developing a reputation for washing fastidiously and dressing with great care and style.

14. The Georgians Drank an Awful Lot of Hot Drinks

Tea and coffee became status symbols. Both were consumed in enormous quantities throughout the period. Coffee shops, which had sprung up the century before, became 'penny universities' where men met, conversed, read the papers and exchanged views. They didn't just sell coffee, they also served tea and chocolate (but never alcohol). Some shops, such as Jonathan's Coffee House, developed into a form of stock exchange, while others, such as Edward Lloyd's Coffee House, specialised in marine insurance. Above all they became centres for news and intelligence about what was going on in the world, with magazines like the *Tatler* and *The Spectator* enjoying a wide circulation.

The taste for coffee was brought into the domestic arena, and became associated with ever more elaborate rituals, using increasingly ostentatious tableware, silver pots, stands and so on. Meanwhile, the ritual of 'taking tea' became increasingly important, with the hostess dispensing with the servants and taking personal charge of the preparation of the brew. She would first mix her own personal blend of green and black teas, bought from shops such as Twinings, which had opened in 1706. The ritual echoed the Chinese tradition, and makers of cups and saucers worked to come up with wares to resemble Chinese porcelain. The thin, almost transparent crockery developed by the Chelsea Porcelain Manufactory in around 1743 was quickly imitated by others, and never was it more important to 'add the milk first', to stop the boiling water from cracking the delicate and fragile cups.

15. Handel Gave Us *Zadok*, *Water Music* and *Messiah*

George Frideric Handel came to London in 1710, aged twenty-four: the first of many immigrants who came to Britain from Germany at the time of the accession of George I. At the time there was an endless demand for Italian operas, and Handel produced music for three separate London opera houses. His orchestral piece *Water Music* was composed in 1717.

Handel wrote four coronation anthems, including *Zadok the Priest* for the coronation of George II in 1727. *Zadok* has been performed at every subsequent coronation. He went on to write some forty-two operas and nearly thirty oratorios. *Messiah*, first performed in Dublin, eventually became one of the most performed pieces of chamber music in history, along with its much-loved 'Hallelujah Chorus'. When he composed *Music for the Royal Fireworks* in 1749, it was performed in front of a crowd of 12,000. In the following year he composed a special arrangement of *Messiah*, performed in support of Thomas Coram's Foundling Hospital. It became an often repeated sell-out benefit concert and he joined the hospital's board of governors.

Handel's early childhood was marked by parental disapproval of his musical aspirations, especially from his father. How ironic then that he should find such success in a foreign country, where he became wealthy and revered and a great philanthropist. Handel died aged seventy-four, in 1759, and was awarded a state funeral at Westminster Abbey. In the opinion of Ludwig van Beethoven, citing *Messiah*, Handel was the 'greatest composer that ever lived'.

16. THE BEGGAR'S OPERA MADE JOHN RICH GAY AND JOHN GAY RICH

The *Beggar's Opera*, written by John Gay and produced by John Rich, was first performed in 1728 at the Lincoln's Inn Fields Theatre. It became a huge success, giving rise to the witticism that it 'made Rich very gay, and Gay very rich'. In a sense it was an 'anti-opera' – an attack on the prevailing fashion in London for operas performed in Italian by Italian sopranos. Instead, Gay gave the public an entertainment which was earthy, bawdy and made use of tunes which were already popular with the general public. Some of the songs were popular ballads, others were based on hymns or folk songs and all were set to tunes people could hum along to. Above all, it was in English, a ballad opera in three parts, featuring characters which the public easily recognised.

On one level, it featured characters from 'the lower orders': a highwayman called Macheath – a character that the audience would immediately have recognised as a mixture of two well-known petty criminals, Jack Sheppard and Jonathan Wild – and Polly Peachum, the 'tart with a heart.' Her part was played by an actress who had done her fair share of horizontal jogging, the prostitute Lavinia Fenton. She so excelled in the part of Polly that she caught the attention of the star-struck Charles Powlett, 3rd Duke of Bolton. His problem was that he was already married, but that didn't stop him from attending every performance and eventually persuading Lavinia to run off with him. When the duke's first wife died, he married her, thereby elevating the whore-who-played-a-whore to the rank of duchess.

On another level, the *Beggar's Opera* was a satirical

attack on the administration of Sir Robert Walpole, who was seen as being corrupt to the core. The play's message was simple: why should the rich get away with corruption and theft from public office, when the lower orders are hounded by the law? To John Gay, both types of immoral behaviour were the same, and the performance ends with a comment from the Beggar (playing the part of narrator) 'that the lower People have their Vices in a Degree as well as the Rich, and are punished for them'. This contrasted with the treatment of Walpole and his wealthy cronies, who were effectively above the law.

The public loved it and the play ran for sixty-two consecutive performances, becoming the most-performed stage production of the eighteenth century. It was constantly revived throughout the 1700s, and had an enormous influence on the operettas of the following century – and indeed on modern musicals.

A follow-up entitled *Polly* and set in the Caribbean was written by Gay in 1729. It was an even more acerbic attack on Sir Robert Walpole, but this time Walpole was able to persuade the Lord Chancellor to ban the performances altogether. *Polly* did not see the light of day on the London stage for another fifty years, but the publicity linked to the censorship helped the sale of printed copies considerably.

17. The Waters of Bath May Have Tasted Foul, but There Were Thousands of Takers

Much of the centre of modern-day Bath was constructed in the Georgian era, using stone quarried from nearby Combe Down. It had been a sleepy little town with Roman origins until the Stuart period, when a doctor by the name of Thomas Guidott wrote a book extolling the curative qualities of Bath's hot water springs. Published in 1676, it led to a trickle of visitors. The trickle then became a flood, so that by 1801 there were more than 40,000 people living in the city.

Bath became an elegant tourist attraction as well as a health spa, and to meet the requirements of the well-heeled visitors more and more fine houses were constructed. Prestigious residences such as those in Queen Square, the Circus and the Royal Crescent were designed by father-and-son architects, both called John Wood. Fine public buildings such as the Assembly Rooms and the Octagon followed in the 1770s. Pulteney Bridge and its weir were constructed to the design of Robert Adam and opened in 1774, and the previous Pump Room was replaced in 1795, the same year the Sydney Gardens opened as a fashionable place to meet, promenade and attend public concerts and entertainments.

What set Bath apart from other resorts was in part down to the efforts of one man, Richard 'Beau' Nash. As Master of Ceremonies he introduced rules of behaviour and established a dress code, which helped Bath become one of the most important marriage markets in the land.

18. Mr Bramah Not Only Invented the Flush Toilet but a Lock to Go with It

In the eighteenth century people generally used a 'close stool' or commode. However, in 1775 a watchmaker called Alexander Cumming patented his design for a pan with a sliding valve at the base, called 'the strap'. The flush toilet was born. Shortly afterwards a young cabinet maker called Joseph Bramah began working with a Mr Allen, installing closets based upon the Cummings patent. Mr Allen decided on a few improvements aimed at stopping the water freezing in cold weather, so he replaced the strap with a hinged flap, sealing the base of the bowl. The credit should go to Allen, but the patent went to young Bramah. He opened a factory in St Giles and poured out quantities of the new-fangled sanitary-wares throughout the next century.

It wasn't long before potters like Josiah Wedgwood got in on the act, designing his first decorated closet pan in 1777. Mind you, there was no sewerage system to go with them, so 'the problem' of the effluent was merely moved further downstream, so to speak.

In 1784 Mr Bramah patented a new type of lock, notable for its resistance to being picked. The Bramah Locks company famously had a 'Challenge Lock' displayed in their London shop window from 1790, mounted on a board with the inscription, 'The artist who can make an instrument that will pick or open this lock shall receive 200 guineas the moment it is produced.' The reward went unclaimed for nearly seventy years.

19. Mr Addis Made Both a Toothbrush and a Fortune

William Addis was born in 1734, and grew up to become a rag trader, living in London's East End. To give him credit for inventing the toothbrush is perhaps a little too strong a statement. After all, the word 'toothbrush' had been around for some time (it first appeared in English in 1690) and the Chinese had been using toothbrushes made from bamboo and hog's hair for hundreds of years. However, in the Western world these had never caught on, and people either used chewing sticks (in effect, twigs which had been chewed to create a splayed end which could be rubbed against the tooth) or rags. Either way, these were used to apply a gentle abrasive such as coal dust, salt, brick dust, etc.

The story goes that in 1780 Addis was thrown into Newgate prison for causing a riot. He got a bit fed up with rubbing his teeth with an old rag and a spot of brick dust and thought he could come up with a better solution; modern oral hygiene was just around the corner. Allegedly, he saved a piece of bone found in his prison meal, drilled half a dozen small holes in one end and, inspired at seeing a broom standing in the corner of his cell, decided to thread horse-hair bristles though the holes. The bristles were then glued or wired into place. Later experiments involved badger hair and hair from the Siberian boar.

Keen to spread the word about oral hygiene (and to make a buck), Addis then started making the brushes commercially from his premises in Whitechapel. He formed a company in 1780 and the brushes were an immediate success. Quantities of ox and bullock thigh bones would be bought from the butchers, minus the ends (which were sold off to be cut into discs by the button makers). The bones, often a couple of feet long, would be boiled, cleaned and cut up lengthwise to make strips, which were then cut to length to make the four different sizes of brush: gents, ladies, children and Tom Thumb. The handles would be shaped to create the head, which was then drilled with holes to hold the bristles.

At this stage in the manufacturing process (and apparently there were some fifty-three separate steps) the blanks would be sent out for 'filling', i.e., securing tight bundles of bristles together, threading them through the drilled holes and cutting them to the required length.

Rather than have a single, large factory (all those nasty overheads!) William Addis followed a system used by many other trades, farming out the filling process to women working from their homes in Spitalfields and Whitechapel, and paying them on a piecework basis. The workers had to supply their own tools and materials. From the company's viewpoint it was great: it meant low overheads, and if the goods were not deemed 'up to the mark' no payment had to be made.

20. Commodore Anson Hijacked a Ship and Brought Home a Fortune

When Commodore Anson set sail in 1740, Britain was at war with Spain. His mission was somewhat ambitious: he was to sail around Cape Horn, harass Spanish shipping in South America, instigate a rebellion in Peru and then head on to capture Panama. He was supposed to have been given 500 soldiers, but what he got was half that number, most of them so infirm and bedridden that they had to be brought on board on stretchers.

The small squadron under Anson's control encountered ferocious storms, and most of the ships were lost. By the time he returned to England nearly four years later, on board his ship *The Centurion*, he had circumnavigated the globe. Out of the original total of 1854 men under his command, only 188 men returned. The rest all perished, either by drowning or as a result of diseases such as scurvy, typhus and dysentery.

But what a return it was. He didn't capture Peru or Panama, but what he did do was intercept the Spanish treasure ship *Covadonga*, laden to the gunwales with silver and gold, off the coast of the Philippines. With minimal casualties, Anson's men seized a vast treasure and sailed for home. The booty included some 1,313,843 pieces of eight. Anson's share of the prize money came to over £90,000. The ordinary seamen under his command got perhaps £300 each. He was made up to admiral, went back to sea and defeated the French fleet at the Battle of Finisterre in 1747. He died in 1762, aged sixty-five.

21. If the Pox Didn't Kill You, the Cure Definitely Would

One feature of the eighteenth century was the uncontrolled explosion in the number of people afflicted by the pox. The word 'pox' (or, more accurately, the Great Pox, to distinguish it from smallpox) was a general term used to describe venereal disease. Doctors made no differentiation between syphilis and gonorrhoea, or any other type of sexually transmitted disease – they were all 'the pox', and it was incurable. Sexual promiscuity, a failure to understand the importance of personal hygiene and the comparative rarity of using condoms, were all factors in the spread of the epidemic. Victims of the pox were likely to suffer from wasting, paralysis and insanity – and that was before mercury took its own toll. Disguising the pock-marked ravages on the face led to the fashion of wearing patches, a fashion accessory adopted by all levels of society, by both women and men.

The condom was widely available but would not have matched modern safety standards, being made from porous animal intestines, usually tied at the end with a pink ribbon. Condoms had the drawback of needing to be immersed in water before being used, in order to make them pliable.

The sex trade was a major employer: there are estimates that one in five women in London was engaged, in some form or other, in the business of offering sex for sale. Prostitution was never a felony in itself, but running a disorderly house was an offence. Bribery and backhanders to constables and magistrates ensured that countless brothels and bathhouses (known as bagnios) flourished, especially in the area around Covent Garden.

At one end of the scale there were the high-class courtesans, who were so in vogue that they could charge a 'signing-on fee' running to many hundreds of pounds. In the middle there were the prostitutes who worked for a madam. Often, she would provide her girls with fine silks so that they could attract well-heeled customers, but the girls would be required to sign promissory notes for a hugely exaggerated sum which they could never repay. These girls would maybe charge a few guineas for their services. At the bottom of the pile were the streetwalkers, willing to offer themselves for a few pennies and a bottle of wine, plying their trade outside the taverns and bawdy houses.

All of them had one thing in common: they were at high risk of contracting a disease which was ultimately a killer, and all of them were led to believe that the best hope of a cure rested with following a course of treatment which had horrific side effects.

Mercury was prescribed as an ointment or as a pill, but it had horrendous effects on the human body. Mouth ulcers, loss of teeth, kidney failure and death by mercury poisoning was the fate of tens of thousands, young and old. As the saying went, 'A night with Venus, and a lifetime with Mercury.'

22. The '45 Rebellion Caused the Nine of Diamonds to Be Known as 'the Curse of Scotland'

The Duke of Cumberland has gone down in history as 'The Butcher of Culloden' – a name bestowed on him by his elder brother, the Prince of Wales, for political reasons. The two did not get on.

To give him his actual name, William Augustus was born in 1721 in London, the third son of George II and Caroline of Ansbach. The title 'Duke of Cumberland' was bestowed on him at five years old. He became a soldier and achieved great popularity for his bravery in the successful Battle of Dettingen (1743), where he was wounded in the leg by a musket ball. He was immediately made a lieutenant general and within two years was placed in command of the combined British, Hanoverian, Austrian and Dutch forces. His inexperience was demonstrated at the Battle of Fontenoy, where he was comprehensively beaten by France's Marshal Maurice de Saxe in May 1745.

Later that year 'the martial boy' was recalled to England to oppose the invasion led by Bonnie Prince Charlie (Charles Edward Stuart, the Young Pretender, grandson of the deposed James II). His appointment was hugely popular, particularly with the troops. Up until then the rebel army had been highly successful in making use of the 'Highland charge'. At the Battle of Prestonpans in September 1745 and the Battle of Falkirk in January 1746, the Highland charge caused havoc against the British Army.

It was with this background that Cumberland marched up to Edinburgh, headed towards Aberdeen and then on to Inverness. By now he had insisted on the Army being trained to combat the Highland charge. The first row of infantry were to hold their fire until the enemy were just twelve yards away. While the front rank reloaded, the second rank fired their guns. By the time the third rank had fired their guns, the first rank were ready to fire again.

Some of the English infantry had the benefit of using the more modern firelocks instead of the older matchlocks, which were slow to reload. Some of their guns had bayonets with which to dispatch any Scotsmen who got too close – no match on their own against the Scottish broadsword, but effective when used in conjunction with this style of fighting.

When the forces met at Culloden Moor near Inverness on 16 April 1746, the Highland charge failed to make its mark. Some 1,000 Scots died. After the battle, Cumberland was purportedly in his tent playing cards. When he was asked for orders, he wrote 'no quarter' on the back of the nine of diamonds – a card still known to this day as the 'curse of Scotland'. The resultant hunting down and indiscriminate killing of men, women and children in the Scottish Highlands left deep scars throughout much of Scotland – although interestingly the good burghers of Glasgow were so pleased with him that they promptly awarded Cumberland an honorary degree.

23. THE '45 REBELLION LED TO THE ORDNANCE SURVEY

After the Battle of Culloden the rebels were chased into their heartland – deep into the Highlands. The English forces were hampered by totally inadequate maps of the area. There were simple linear maps showing the route between principal towns and cities, but nothing showing the topography, or the more remote areas.

The king commissioned a full military survey of the Scottish Highlands in 1746, overseen by a young engineer called William Roy. Roy's vision was for a military survey covering the entire country, and although it wasn't implemented until after his death in 1790, war with France and the threat of invasion propelled his ideas into the limelight. The Board of Ordnance began a survey of England's vulnerable southern coasts.

The task coincided with the invention of an instrument essential to accurate surveying: the theodolite. In 1784 an order was placed with the Yorkshire-born instrument-maker and inventor Jesse Ramsden. It took three years to build. A second theodolite was delivered in 1791. This enabled the cartographers to establish a baseline and to carry out a survey known as the Principal Triangulation of Great Britain. The first Ordnance Survey Map appeared in 1801, covering the county of Kent. Within twenty years a third of the country had been mapped, at a scale of one inch to the mile. Ironically, the one inch to a mile maps had to be withdrawn between 1811 and 1816, for fear that they would be of use to the enemy in the event of a French invasion.

24. THE '45 REBELLION ALSO HELPED IMPROVE OUR ROADS

Marching the British Army north to meet the threat from Bonnie Prince Charlie proved a nightmare for the forces under the command of the Duke of Cumberland. The roads were in an appalling state – deeply rutted and almost impassable for heavy waggons. Their axles broke, causing long delays while repairs were effected. After the rebellion a report was handed into Parliament, and this led directly to an explosion in the use of the turnpike trusts. These local bodies were formed with the express purpose of upgrading roads in a particular vicinity. Each one necessitated a private Act of Parliament, and gave the trustees the power to erect a toll-keeper's cottage alongside the turnpike gates, at which tolls would be imposed.

Turnpikes got their name from a barrier made of upright pikes secured with a horizontal bar, which could be rotated to allow free passage. First used in the Stuart period, after 1745 their use expanded greatly. By 1750 there were some 150 trusts; by 1825 roughly 18,000 miles of road in England and Wales were under the control of a thousand turnpike trusts. By the end of the Georgian period nearly a fifth of all roads had been turnpiked, and the improvements helped transform commerce, enabling goods to be transported swiftly and easily across the country.

New road-making techniques were introduced by engineers such as John McAdam and Thomas Telling, and before long road improvements reached the stage where travel at night became feasible for long-distance coaches.

25. At 282 Days, 1751 Was the Shortest Year on Record

In the first half of the eighteenth century there were several different calendars in use. France and most of Western Europe had switched to the Gregorian calendar (named after Pope Gregory), whereas Britain still used the Julian calendar (named after Julius Caesar). To add to the confusion, Russia had its own method of calculating the date. The lack of conformity led to all sorts of difficulties for travellers and for any businesses trading with Europe.

Fearing anything which might be associated with the Catholic papacy, the British government had resisted changing to the Gregorian calendar, but being out of sync with Europe was a pain in the neck. The problem was that the government wanted to adopt the change without ever having to use the word 'Gregorian' or imply that they were in any way following a papal directive. However, a decision was made to come into line with the rest of Europe, and The Calendar Act was passed in 1750. Pope Gregory's name is never mentioned in the Act, which had two significant effects.

The first was to alter the date when the old year ended. For centuries the changeover of the legal year had been 25 March, making 26 March New Year's Day. In popular use, New Year's Day had long been 1 January, so the change merely brought the lawyers in line with what was already accepted practice. Legal documents for some years had to include two dates, one old style, and the other new style, to make it clear what year was actually involved. The change came into effect in 1751, and therefore that year ran from 26 March to 31 December. The following day was

1 January 1752, meaning that 1751 lasted only 282 days.

That was only half the story, although at least it brought us into line with Scotland, which had changed its year on 1 January since 1600. However, it still left us out of step with most European countries, because the Julian calendar, based on the thirty-day lunar cycle, dealt inadequately with leap years.

The difficulty arose because a solar year is slightly less than 365.25 days, and therefore a leap day, rigidly applied every four years, led to inaccuracies. The shortfall added up over the years, at roughly three whole days every four centuries, and the Gregorian calendar took this discrepancy into account by ditching those three days every 400 years. Our Julian calendar did not have this arrangement, and our dates were behind those in Europe. Parliament solved the problem by leap-frogging eleven days. This meant that people went to bed on Wednesday 2 September 1752, and woke up the next day on Thursday 14 September. As a result of the change, 1752 was shortened to a mere 355 days. Confused? One story goes that people took to the streets demanding, 'Give us back our eleven days,' but in all probability this is apocryphal.

26. The Seven Years War Didn't Last Seven Years

The Seven Years War actually lasted nine years, having started as a conflict between the English and the French in North America in 1754. Two years later it escalated into the world's first truly global war, bringing in all of the major European powers and spreading from Europe to the Caribbean, West Africa and India. By the time the Treaty of Paris was signed in 1763, more than a million people had been killed in the fighting, which left Britain very much top of the pile. British gains were mostly at the expense of the French, nowhere more so than in Canada.

Up until that time, the French dominated the areas around Montreal and Quebec, but that ended in 1759, described at the time as the *annus mirabilis* or 'year of wonders', when the British won victories over the French on every continent. Until that time the British forces in North America had met with mixed success, with the French combining successfully with the Native Canadian groups living in the Laurentian valley. William Pitt the Elder recognised the importance of the area to Britain's colonial expansion and sent General Wolfe with orders to capture Quebec and drive the French out of Canada. After success at the Siege of Louisbourg, Wolfe moved upriver to Quebec and laid siege to the heavily fortified town, which occupied high ground above the river. The French easily repulsed the early attacks. After numerous changes of plan, Wolfe ordered a diversionary feint while ordering his men to scale a steep slope which the French commander Montcalm had left only lightly defended. The cliff was some 200 metres high and the assault needed to be carried out under cover of darkness. The plan worked, and the morning of 13 September saw Wolfe assemble his troops on the Plains of Abraham, in an impregnable position above the city. Montcalm brought his troops out to face the enemy, leading to a battle which was effectively over in the space of fifteen minutes. In that time, Wolfe was hit by three musket shots, and he died on the spot. Montcalm was also mortally wounded, but was carried from the battlefield and died the following day. The French withdrew behind the city gates, but their position was untenable and the garrison quickly surrendered. From there the British forces advanced on Montreal, and within a year France had lost control throughout the whole of North America, with the exception of Louisiana.

Someone once described Wolfe to George II as being mad, eliciting the comment, 'Mad, is he? Then I hope he will bite some of my other generals.' In death he became an iconic figure and inspired a whole nation. His body was brought back from Canada and in November 1759 was interred at Greenwich. The day of the funeral saw the last of the year's major victories over the French, with Admiral Hawke defeating their fleet in the Battle of Quiberon Bay.

27. Clive Was Amazed at His Own Moderation

Robert Clive, born in 1725, went on to become 1st Baron Clive but was generally known as Clive of India. He helped establish British control in India, was an inspiring leader and a great administrator. He also made himself extremely rich. When he returned to England as a thirty-five-year-old, he had already amassed a fortune of £300,000. Years later, Parliament sought to review the conduct of the East India Company, and proceedings developed into little more than a thinly disguised attack on Clive personally. Parliament accused him of lining his own pockets, to which he responded, 'I stand astonished at my own moderation.' Clive was eventually exonerated and ended up being commended for his 'great and meritorious service' to the country.

He had originally gone to India as a clerk in the East India Company, reaching Madras (now Chennai) in 1744, at a time when the East India Company had only half a dozen trading posts throughout the entire subcontinent. There was constant friction between the company and its French counterparts, and a *de facto* guerrilla war broke out between the two sides. It turned out to be a form of warfare at which the astute Robert Clive proved to be especially adept.

In 1756 he was sent to Bengal, at that time ruled by viceroys on behalf of the Mughal emperor. By the time he got there the fort at Calcutta had fallen to the rebel Nawab of Bengal, causing a complete interruption to the trading activities of the East India Company. It also led to the infamous atrocity known as the Black Hole of Calcutta in which 123 British prisoners were alleged to have died. At the start of 1757 Calcutta was recaptured by Clive. He went on to win the Battle of Plassey, with the loss of less than two dozen men, gaining a victory which left him in control of almost the whole of Bengal. Other victories and political alliances followed. As a result, Clive was able to secure for himself a cash reward of over £234,000, a Mughal title of nobility and an estate giving him an annual income of almost £30,000. He also secured for the East India Company hugely favourable trading terms and £1.5 million in compensation for losses linked to the earlier capture of Calcutta. Clive returned to Britain in 1760 and became an MP, being knighted four years later.

On his return to India in 1765 he was faced with mounting problems of corruption and bureaucracy throughout the bloated East India Company. He tackled the problem with great enthusiasm and ended up streamlining both the administration and the army. In doing so he made many enemies. He returned to Britain but suffered increasingly from depression. He took his own life, aged forty-nine, in 1774, but goes down in history as the man who helped establish the British Empire. The Raj would never have been possible without men like Clive.

28. The State Lottery Existed Long Before Camelot

State lotteries were popular in the eighteenth century. Often such lotteries were used to raise money for specific 'good causes', such as the construction of the new bridge across the Thames at Westminster, or the establishment of the British Museum at Montagu House. Even military campaigns were part-funded by the State lottery.

The background to each lottery was that the government would agree to pay a specific sum of money on a particular date as prize money. That total would be sub-divided into £10 shares, which would be bought by various lottery offices, typically for £16 each, giving the government a generous profit. Each lottery-office keeper would then split the shares into fractions, from one-half to one-sixteenth, and offer these to the public on the basis of one whole share having a face value of £25. A number of blanks would be added, helping to bump up the profits. The exact number of blanks was declared in advance. Players could insure against a blank being drawn, usually by paying a fee to a 'Moroccan' – in other words, a spiv offering odds and wielding a red Moroccan purse in which he kept the money he earned. Alternatively punters could go into the lottery insurance office to take out insurance against a blank being drawn. For example, the 1775 State lottery involved 60,000 tickets, of which 40,000 were blank and 20,000 were eligible for a prize. In other words, there was a one-in-three-chance of winning a prize of some sort. The majority of winners got £15, but the maximum prize was £20,000.

The actual tickets were printed as an original and

a counterpart, divided by a row of perforations. One half was handed to the buyer and the other was retained by the lottery-office keeper until the day of the draw. Considerable razzmatazz was attached to the great ceremony of choosing the winning tickets. Initially the selection was made at London's Guildhall, but later this changed to Cooper's Hall in Basinghall Street. On the day prior to the lottery, all the tickets would be collected and taken to Somerset House. Three chests would be on public display. Into one went the blanks, into another the prizes and into the third box went the printed tickets. With much ceremony, the boxes would then be locked with seven keys and seals, and in a flurry of showmanship they would be paraded through the streets, along with three wheels of fortune, under the watchful eye of the Horse Guards, to the place where the draw was to take place. The public could watch as the tickets were put into one or other of the two wheels of fortune, which would be spun round. Two young boys would simultaneously dip in a hand and draw out a ticket, which the 'lottery proclaimer' would read out, matching the number with either a prize or a blank, in a ceremony which could take many hours.

29. The Lunar Society Had Lunarticks as Members

The Lunar Society of Birmingham (originally called the Lunar Circle) was a dinner club which got its name because it met on the Monday night closest to the date of the full moon. This was done for the eminently sensible reason that members could thereby see their way home after the meeting, despite a lack of street lighting. It had fourteen core members at any given time, but these were allowed to invite guests, and they all happily adopted the name 'lunarticks' to describe their nocturnal activities. Its heyday was between 1765 and 1789, and for much of the time members met at Soho House, home to the industrialist Matthew Boulton. Meetings were also held at the home of Erasmus Darwin in Lichfield, at Bowbridge House in Derbyshire and at Great Barr Hall.

What set it apart from other groups was that this particular gathering of businessmen attracted the very cream of the Midlands Enlightenment. Headed by Boulton, it included the poet, inventor and botanist Erasmus Darwin (grandfather of Charles) and also the potter Josiah Wedgwood. Another member was the clockmaker and inventor John Whitehurst, who would come and stay at Soho House in order to demonstrate new discoveries and inventions. James Watt was on hand to put forward his ideas for the future of steam power, aided by the brilliant engineer William Murdoch, while Joseph Priestley was no doubt able to talk about his discovery of fizzy drinks (or rather, carbonated water). Benjamin Franklin came as a guest on more than one occasion, bringing with him demonstrations involving electrical experiments, while the Swiss inventor Argand came to discuss his ideas for balloons and his designs for a gas lamp which was to light up homes throughout the nineteenth century. Thomas Jefferson, Sir Richard Arkwright and John Smeaton were also invited as guests, bringing with them their own ideas about how society could benefit from the latest discoveries.

The revolution in France was followed two years later by rioting in Birmingham on 4 July 1791. The homes of various members were targeted, especially that of Joseph Priestley, because he was seen as a supporter of the revolution. His laboratory was smashed up, his wine cellar emptied and his home set ablaze. He had sensibly left the scene and moved to the United States. Erasmus Darwin had already gone to live in Derby, and age took its toll on the Lunar Society membership. By 1791 the activities and influence of the society started to wane, and within a decade it was dominated by the sons of the original members. It effectively finished in 1813. In its time it helped develop new ideas in science, agriculture, manufacturing, transport and mining, and as such contributed significantly to the Industrial Revolution. Nowadays its activities would be termed 'networking', a sort of think tank. In the eighteenth century it was just a group of men who dreamed of changing the world, and then went out and did just that.

30. Print Shops Helped Turn the Famous into Celebrities

In 1777 a woman called Hannah Humphrey opened a shop in London selling prints, generally caricatures, based on etchings made by contemporary artists. She was by no means the first. Mary and Matthew Darly, a husband-and-wife team, had opened three separate shops in central London, specialising in the sale of prints poking fun at the followers of macaroni fashions. Hannah started to sell works by James Gillray, a young man with vitriolic views and a savage line in social commentary. In 1791 James moved in with Hannah and remained her partner for twenty years. During that time the partnership grew to symbolise a remarkable feature of the last quarter of the century: the importance of the print shop and the growth of visual satire. In France and America revolutions overthrew monarchies. In England, caricaturists helped the public let off steam, ridiculing King George III and his family, but equally poking fun at his ministers, the aristocracy, the clergy, lawyers and authority in general.

Politics was dominated by partisan rivalries between the Tories (identified with William Pitt the Younger) and the Whigs (led by Charles James Fox). Gillray satirised both – Pitt as a pipe-cleaner-thin, scrawny weakling, and Fox as a gambling rake with a six o'clock shadow. Gillray was no friend of either political party and was savage in his condemnation of all human folly of whatever political persuasion. Equally, he was quite happy to be bought off and to accept a government pension in return for agreeing not to attack the party in power. On some occasions, entire print runs were bought up by the unhappy 'victim', anxious to protect his or her reputation and to remain out of the public gaze. Gillray was happy to be censored as long as he got paid handsomely.

Others followed in Gillray's path, most notably the somewhat dissolute Thomas Rowlandson. He was known to eat and drink to excess, and to spend up to thirty-six hours at a time at the gaming tables. He was a trained artist, having attended the Royal Academy, and his drawings helped propel caricatures into an art form which has never been equalled. Some of his works were positively top-shelf, being somewhat pornographic and very much intended to be collected privately rather than exhibited in shop windows. Another caricaturist was Richard Newton, who displayed a typical teenager's love of all things crude and indecent. He died tragically at the age of twenty-one, thereby denying the world of the benefit of his humour and artistry. The Cruikshanks, father and son, developed the satirical tradition well into the nineteenth century.

The caricaturists succeeded in bringing individuals under public scrutiny. Suddenly, the general public could see what their social superiors looked like: they knew their portraits, could identify with the people being lampooned and could laugh at the situations which corrupt politicians got themselves into. They could buy the prints and hang them on their walls at home. It marked the birth of modern celebrity.

31. Cosmetics Were to Die For

Eighteenth-century writers such as Jonathan Swift were forever banging on about how unfair it was that women used make-up: that it was a deception which meant that men could not tell what was false and what was real. Nonetheless, throughout the century women seemed addicted to applying heavy make-up to their faces, even though they knew the consequences could be fatal.

Most of the cosmetics contained lead, which became toxic over time, especially when applied to open sores and abrasions. Symptoms of lead poisoning include severe headaches, sickness, dizziness and blindness. If consumed in large-enough quantities, it can lead to paralysis and even death. Despite this, women were slaves to the fashion and slapped it on by the handful.

One high-profile case of lead poisoning involved the famous beauty Maria Gunning, who died of it in 1760, at the age of twenty-seven. For years she had been applying liberal quantities of ceruse to whiten her skin. This compound of lead oxide, hydroxide and carbonate proved to be a lethal cocktail, as the hydroxide and carbonate combined with the moisture in her skin to form acids which slowly ate it away. While she was alive her husband had taken a mistress, the famous courtesan Kitty Fisher. She too was slavishly dedicated to the fashion of alabaster-white skin, and died at much the same age (although the pox or tuberculosis may have played a part in her death). Even in death Kitty cared for her looks: she directed that she be buried wearing her best ballgown!

White lead lay at the heart of the problem. It was obtained as a flaky, white powder after sheets of lead coated in vinegar had been submerged in a pit of manure for a few weeks. The chemical reaction of the vinegar on the lead turned it white and soft. It could then be ground up and mixed with water. Finally, perfume and tinting dye would be added and – hey presto! – it was ready to be slathered on the face, neck and upper chest. Veins across the bust would be enhanced with blueish lines, while the whiteness of the face was accentuated by the addition of circles of rouge. However, rouge was also derived from a lead-based product, and despite other cosmetics being based on harmless herbal ingredients or mixed with honey, they could not counteract the harm being done by the lead.

The fashion was for small, bee-stung (rosebud) lips, and colour might be applied by both men and women. This involved more lead-based products, sometimes with the addition of mercury and arsenic. Colours ranged from bright-red to pink, and were applied with a pad of colour-impregnated wool or hair, called Spanish wool. This red effect could also be achieved by dabbing vinegar or distilled alcohol onto the lips. By the middle of the eighteenth century, coloured lip balms became available, made from a mixture of carmine and plaster of Paris.

Small wonder make-up was known as 'paint'!

32. John Wesley Agreed to Disagree

When John Wesley was born, in 1703, to Samuel and Susanna Wesley in Epworth, Lincolnshire, he was their fifteenth child. His mother went on to have four more children. When he was five years old the family home caught fire, and he had to be rescued from an upstairs window by a parishioner standing on the shoulders of a neighbour. As he was afterwards wont to say, he was 'a brand plucked out of the fire'. He went on to be educated at Charterhouse and Christ Church, Oxford, and eventually became the founder of the evangelical movement known as Methodism.

He was made a fellow of Lincoln College, Oxford, in 1726. Here he taught Greek and established the Holy Club, dubbed 'Methodist' due to its members' prescribed method of studying the Bible. He was ordained into the priesthood in 1728 and at that stage there was little to mark out this deeply religious young man from many others in the Church of England. Yet within a few years he was branded a troublemaker, a rabble-rouser and a danger to the established order. Vicars were supposed to 'stick to their own' parishes. Wesley did not, and in 1739 followed the example of his friend, the evangelist George Whitfield, by addressing an open-air congregation just outside Bristol. This became known as 'field preaching'.

For many years, the common people had felt little affinity with the Church of England; it did not speak their language and it did not express their concerns. But the passionate Wesley *did* speak their language, and he did care about their poverty, their unjust treatment, their poor housing and their bad working conditions. People flocked to hear what he had to say. He travelled extensively throughout Britain and Ireland, as well as crossing the Atlantic in order to develop small Christian-study groups. These were led by non-ordained evangelists, appointed personally by Wesley.

Over his lifetime he is thought to have delivered some 40,000 sermons and to have travelled 250,000 miles in the process. He spoke out against slavery and demanded prison reform, universal education and social change. He set up a network of lay preachers, both in Britain and in America. Chapels were opened, and he introduced a system of itinerancy whereby preachers were expected to preach at different venues within their circuit, at a rate of no fewer than thirty occasions each month. Wesley opened schools, administered charities and led the Methodist movement until his death in 1791. He was a vegetarian, abstained from drinking wine and advocated the use of electricity for its curative properties. When Whitfield died, Wesley delivered a sermon in which he referred to their doctrinal differences. As he put it, 'they agreed to disagree' – the first time this saying appeared in print. In an age of religious bigotry, he stood out as a man who was big enough to tolerate the views of others. In death, he was described as 'the best loved man in England'.

33. James Cook Never Lived to Enjoy Valentine's Day

Cook was one of those rarities: a seaman who rose through the ranks. During his naval career he embarked on three major world voyages, circumnavigated New Zealand and helped put Australia on the map. In doing so, he greatly increased knowledge of the world by mapping thousands of miles of previously uncharted ocean.

James was born in a small Yorkshire village in 1728, into a farming family. He joined the merchant navy when he was seventeen, but enlisted in the Royal Navy in 1755. He made a name for himself surveying the shallows in the Saint Lawrence River, making possible General Wolfe's attack on Quebec. The accuracy of his surveying, often in very difficult conditions, brought him to the attention of the government. The Royal Society wanted a small fleet to head to the Pacific to watch the transit of Venus. The idea was to take exact measurements, at different fixed points in the world, of the time taken for Venus to pass in front of the sun, so that it would be possible to measure precisely the distance between Venus and Earth.

Cook, then aged thirty-nine, was made up to lieutenant and put in charge of the expedition, which left England in August 1768. Eight months later the transit was observed in Tahiti. At that point Cook opened the second part of his sealed orders: sail south and search for the fabled land of Terra Australis. He located New Zealand and mapped its entire coastline, before heading west and reaching the south-eastern coast of Australia. Here he landed at a place that he named Botany Bay, on account of its rich and varied flora and fauna, before heading north and mapping parts of the Great Barrier Reef. He returned home in 1771 to great national excitement, but the hero's welcome was reserved for botanist Joseph Banks, whose drawings and observations had captured the public imagination.

A year later, promoted to commodore, he set off again in the *Enterprise* in search of the mythical continent of Terra Australis. He explored vast areas of the southern ocean, crossing the Antarctic Circle and almost reaching Antarctica, before heading for Tahiti to replenish supplies. He returned to Britain in 1775, having proved conclusively that the Terra Australis myth was just that – a myth. Most significantly, he had been able to test John Harrison's H4 marine chronometer. Measuring longitude had always been a problem for navigators on long voyages, but for the first time this chronometer enabled Cook to calculate his position at sea with great accuracy. Of equal importance, he completed the second voyage without losing a single man to scurvy, thanks to his insistence on his men consuming vegetables and fresh fruit, or, if these items were not available, drinking spruce beer.

Cook set off on a third voyage, looking for the Northwest Passage, but he was killed in Hawaii by angry islanders during an altercation on the beach on 14 February 1779.

34. COAL WAS KING WHEN GEORGE WAS ON THE THRONE

Fortunes were made by landowners lucky enough to have coal under their land. Improved mining techniques enabled shafts to be dug deeper and deeper. There was a certain irony in the fact that deeper mining meant a risk of flooding, a problem overcome by installing machine-operated pumps; the pumps ran on steam power, which was produced by burning coal brought up from ever deeper mines.

Much of the coal was brought into the Port of London, giving rise to the name 'sea coal' because that was how it was transported. Originally, it may have meant that the coal had been mined from tunnels driven out under the seabed from the shoreline, but most sea coal was in fact obtained from land-based mines. Coal output rose dramatically throughout the Georgian era, with around 6.25 million tons being extracted in the decade after 1770. Deep-shaft mining was predominantly practised in Lancashire, Yorkshire and South Wales.

Steam-powered engines were initially used to drive the winding gear, enabling the coal to be brought to the surface. Later, static steam engines were used to pull coal trucks up hills on metal tracks, via cables. Eventually, the steam engines developed into locomotives, such as those designed by Richard Trevethick in 1804, which hauled trucks along a tramway at the Penydarren Ironworks, in Merthyr Tydfil, Wales.

Steam had been used a century earlier to drive pumping engines designed by Thomas Newcomen; over 125 machines were in use by 1730. The machines were inefficient and would not work at any significant depth, and it was left to James Watt to come up with the improvements needed to drive water from the deeper shafts.

There was, of course, always a risk of underground explosions, linked to the build-up of methane and other gases, called firedamp. Historically, fires were lit to create the air currents needed to prevent the build-up of methane, sometimes with disastrous effects. In time, steam power was used to drive fans that created air currents. Matters eventually improved with the invention of the Davy Lamp in 1815. The lamp, invented by Sir Humphry Davy, contained a safety mesh that prevented the candle flame from igniting any methane or other gas, with the added bonus that the flame changed colour if methane was present. The light given out was, however, very weak. The irony is that initially the safety lamp led to more deaths, as mine-owners tried to reopen shafts which had previously been abandoned because they were known to be affected by methane.

Shafts were driven deep underground using pit props (used for the first time after 1800), sometimes reaching depths of over 1,000 feet. Coal production soared from around 3 million tons a year in 1700, to ten times that amount by the end of the Georgian period. Pit collapses were common, and throughout the nineteenth century an average of 1,000 miners died underground every year.

35. The East India Company Was a Superpower in Its Own Right

The East India Company, often informally called John Company, was a joint-stock trading company with origins dating back to 1600. Throughout the Stuart period it had grown steadily, with trading interests particularly linked to the import of highly valued products such as spices, cotton and silk. For many years, a monopoly was formed whereby the East India Company supplied saltpetre, an ingredient which was vital to the making of gunpowder, to the British government.

The import of tea also proved to be a highly profitable monopoly, and the growth in the volume of trade was phenomenal. In 1701 around 120,000 pounds of tea were imported via the East India Company. By 1750 this had increased to 3 million pounds of tea, which was dwarfed in turn by 1801, when importation had increased tenfold to over 31 million pounds.

Another highly lucrative monopoly was linked to opium, which was grown in Bengal and then exported into China, either by smugglers, or by trading agencies linked to the company. The Chinese banned opium imports in 1799, but by then the lucrative and now illegal trade involved some 900 tons of opium being brought into China each year. Protecting the trade route led to the company founding the Straits Settlements in 1826, which combated pirates in the area of the Straits of Malacca. By the end of the Georgian period, opium exports to China were running at 1,400 tons yearly.

By 1720, 15 per cent of all the imports brought into Britain came through the hands of the East India Company. The organisation grew into something of a superpower; its own private armies enabled it to control virtually the whole of India. By 1750, military numbers had reached 3,000, and these escalated to 67,000 by 1778. The stunning military victories of Clive of India, mentioned earlier, made the company a world power. This brought it into regular conflict with Parliament, which was forever trying to clip the wings of this enormous trade leviathan.

The area of land controlled by the company was far too great for one organisation to manage effectively, leading to corruption and neglect. This was particularly borne out by the great famine of 1770, when it is said that one-third of the entire population of Bengal died of starvation. Its riches had been plundered to such an extent that the people could not afford to feed themselves. William Pitt the Younger was responsible for bringing in two pieces of legislation which limited the powers of the company and made it more accountable to Parliament: the Regulating Act of 1773 and Pitt's India Act of 1784. The British government took away its trading monopoly in 1813, and after 1834 it operated as a government agency. The company survived until the Indian Rebellion in 1857, after which it was abolished. Thereafter, the Crown took over direct control of India, in what became known as the British Raj.

36. Laudanum Addicts Gave Way to Cokeheads

Not all of the opium controlled by the East India Company ended up in China: it helped fuel an increasing demand for the opiate back in Britain. In his younger days, Christopher Wren experimented with the effects of taking opium. When he wasn't busy designing churches and cathedrals, Wren found time to inject dogs with the drug. They fell asleep, so he apparently moved on to injecting 'the delinquent servant of a Foreign Minister' (without explaining what the foreign minister thought of it, or why he was employing delinquent servants in the first place). The tests were inconclusive, but what they demonstrated was that opium was available in the late-seventeenth century, and enquiring brains were keen to find out how it worked and what it did to the human mind. In the hundred years that followed, far more was discovered about the remarkable substance, and it became used with greater frequency than ever before. In the days before painkillers or anti-depressants, it was a godsend.

The discovery by the German chemist Friedrich Sertürner of the most common alkaloid of opium, which became known as morphine, occurred in 1804. By 1827 it was being sold commercially in pharmacies, and the invention of the hypodermic syringe in 1857 led to more general usage. The name morphine came from Morpheus, the Greek god of dreams. Codeine, another alkaloid of opium, was discovered by a French chemist in 1835. Throughout the previous century, however, the public had been buying increasing quantities of laudanum. This was a tincture of opium, containing about 1 per cent morphine and taken in liquid form. It formed part of many patent medicines and could be bought without prescription. Poorer people favoured it because, unlike alcohol, laudanum was treated as a medicine and was not taxed. In its original seventeenth-century form it was mixed with alcohol and other substances. Later, it became an essential painkiller, a soporific, an aid to reduce stomach pains and menstrual cramps and an antidote for coughs, colds, cardiac diseases and even yellow fever. Sufferers of gout, such as the Prince Regent, ingested it in increasing quantities in order to relieve their constant pain. It was, of course, highly addictive. Artists and writers took laudanum to help them with their art – Keats wrote of 'emptying some dull opiate to the drains' (in other words, swallowing it). Samuel Taylor Coleridge claimed that he wrote almost all of his poem 'Kubla Khan' while in a drug-induced sleep (at least, until he was disturbed 'by a man from Porlock'), while Thomas de Quincey's *Confessions of an English Opium-Eater*, published in 1821, gave a detailed autobiographical account of the writer's penchant for taking laudanum combined with alcohol. Laudanum was mixed with just about anything and everything – not only alcohol, but hashish, pepper, chloroform, belladonna and even mercury. By 1855, however, science had isolated the alkaloid cocaine from coca leaves, and suddenly drug users were spoilt for choice.

37. George III May Not Have Been Mad to Start with, but He Was by the End

It has been fashionable to explain the various bouts of illness that affected George III throughout his reign as being caused by porphyria. Certainly, one of the symptoms of porphyria can be blue urine, apparently noted by the king's doctors, but others argue that the discolouration was caused by his medicinal use of the gentian root. Nowadays he would probably be diagnosed as suffering from bipolar disorder.

Whatever the cause, the fact remains that the behaviour of the king was at times extremely erratic. Contemporaries speak of his excessive loquacity, which could lead to him literally frothing at the mouth. He would scribble long sentences, only occasionally bothering to use a verb, and spend hours designing enormous palaces, filled with dramatic staircases, but largely devoid of windows. Sometimes he had convulsions and had to be physically restrained by his courtiers. During these bouts of illness he would seek recovery and recuperation at Kew Palace, near Richmond.

Naturally, state business was severely handicapped during the periods when the king was ill. On several occasions, Parliament was on the brink of appointing a regent to rule on the king's behalf, but each time the situation got critical, the monarch recovered. This was particularly true in 1789, when the Regency Bill was passed by both houses. The king was in no fit state to give the Royal Assent, and the Great Seal of the Realm was affixed by the Lord Chancellor, but before the validity of this could be tested in court, the king made a full recovery.

The Prince of Wales was ever-impatient to take over from his father, and gathered around him politicians who saw that they could benefit from such a change. Finally, the complete breakdown in the king's mental state in 1810 meant a decision could no longer be put off. His latest bout of illness was probably triggered by acute depression caused by the death of Princess Amelia, the youngest of his daughters and the apple of his eye. George became increasingly agitated and ended up in a straight-jacket, having to be given medicine by force, against his will. For once, the prince did not overplay his hand by courting the Whig opposition. He bided his time and in due course was rewarded. Parliament, under the leadership of Spencer Perceval, again passed the Regency Bill. The king made no objection to it, giving the Royal Assent, so the Act came into force in 1811. Finally, in a ceremony at Carlton House, the elaborately bedecked Prince of Wales became regent, swearing to be 'faithful and bear true allegiance' to the king; to maintain 'the safety, honour and dignity' of the king and 'the welfare of his people'; and to uphold the Protestant religion.

The regency lasted nine years. During this time George III lived at Windsor Castle. By the end, he was stone deaf, completely blind and utterly insane.

38. The Chippendales Were Considered Wooden, but Polished.

There were in fact two Thomas Chippendales: father and son. The elder Thomas was a Yorkshireman, born in Otley in 1718 to a family with long woodworking and timber-trade traditions. After a spell working as a journeyman carpenter, he moved to London, and, in 1748, he married and went on to father five boys and four girls. In 1754, Thomas moved to fashionable premises at 60–62 St Martin's Lane, where his business remained for sixty years.

Chippendale went into partnership with a wealthy Scottish businessman called James Rannie, enabling him to concentrate on his masterpiece, *The Gentleman and Cabinet Maker's Director*. It contained 161 engraved plates of 'elegant and useful designs of Household Furniture in the Gothic Chinese and Modern Taste', and was a runaway success. Further editions quickly followed. *The Director* was important, because it was the first time a publication had appeared listing designs for others to copy. Its success meant that the Chippendale name became synonymous with the rococo style, although by no means were all the pieces called 'Chippendale' made by him. He employed some fifty in-house carpenters and any number of outworkers. His designs, nearly always involving mahogany, helped consign earlier oak and walnut furniture to the attic; mahogany became the must-have wood for all fashionable establishments.

His role was as artistic director, dealing with wealthy clients and supervising the workforce. Ideally, he preferred to be given commissions to design the furniture for grand houses, from top to bottom, but he also sold 'off the peg' items to the passing trade. Rannie died in 1766. His share in the business was sold to the firm's accountant, Thomas Haig, and for a time the business was known as Chippendale, Haig & Co. With passing years, the elder Thomas Chippendale had less to do with the business – he remarried in 1776 and had two more children, by which time his role had passed to Thomas Chippendale the younger. The old boy moved to Hoxton and died there of tuberculosis in November 1778.

This left the younger Thomas to soldier on until 1803. It must have been a difficult time for Thomas junior, because Haig was the senior partner. When Haig died that year there were insufficient funds to pay his legacies; Thomas was forced to sell up and was declared bankrupt in 1804. He died in 1822.

Thomas Sheraton and George Hepplewhite followed the Chippendale example of producing designs for others to copy. Sheraton, with his four-part *Cabinet-Maker and Upholsterers' Drawing Book,* greatly influenced the neoclassical designs that gained popularity both in Britain and in America, while Hepplewhite made up 'the big three' furniture makers. Very little is known about his life, and no examples of his work can be identified with any certainty. His *Cabinet Maker and Upholsterers Guide* was published by his widow in 1778, two years after his death. Hepplewhite popularised the shield-backed chair and helped move furniture towards a lighter, more elegant style.

39. One Man Can Claim to Have Been the Father of Civil Engineering

John Smeaton was born in 1724, and went on to become the country's first civil engineer. John cut his teeth on windmills and waterwheels, working out their power and effectiveness scientifically, and making improvements to designs which had stood unchanged for centuries. He analysed steam engines, making improvements to the early Newcomen engines and working out ways to measure their performance accurately; he designed bridges and canals; and he advised on schemes for harbours and coastal protection walls.

In 1753 he was admitted to the Royal Society, and six years later was awarded the Copley Medal. It was the Royal Society which recommended Smeaton, then aged thirty, to be the engineer in charge of rebuilding the Eddystone Lighthouse after the previous structure burned down in a disastrous fire.

He studied the physics of cement, not only coming up with a mixture which was quick-drying and could be used underwater, but also setting out the principles which would eventually lead to modern Portland cement. He worked out a way to dovetail solid granite blocks, pegged with marble, to create a structure which could withstand the full force of the sea. He then devised a scheme to raise these blocks 18 metres in the air, from a moving (floating) base so that they could be put in place atop the Eddystone Lighthouse. It was a remarkable achievement and remained in position from 1759 until 1877, when it was dismantled and reassembled, minus its plinth, on Plymouth Hoe.

In the 1760s and '70s he moved on to designing

bridges, viaducts, jetties and harbour walls the length and breadth of the country. In carrying out this wide range of work, he declared that it was different to that carried out by military engineers and named his area of expertise 'civil engineering' to mark that difference. In many senses he can therefore be described as the father of civil engineering. He was both a product of the Industrial Revolution and one of its greatest architects.

His experiments with pumping compressed air into a diving bell, so as to enable workers to operate underwater, were put to use in 1790 during the construction of the breakwater at Ramsgate Harbour. He also designed scientific instruments and helped instil in his pupils that one, over-riding question: how does this work, and what can be done to make it more efficient?

He pioneered fixed fees for routine commissions: 25 guineas for a watermill and 30 guineas for a windmill. Customers were charged 1 guinea for a consultation at his home near Leeds, double that 'if sent for' and 5 guineas if he was required to spend the day in London, a place he loathed.

In 1771 he became one of the founder members of the Society of Civil Engineers – a fortnightly dining club for engineers and scientists to meet and discuss current ideas. It is now known as the Smeatonian Society.

40. Josiah Wedgwood Was Definitely Not Potty

A standout figure of the Georgian period was Josiah Wedgwood, the eleventh child of a family that had been making pots for four generations. He was born in 1730, and his father died when Josiah was seven. He left school two years later and was apprenticed to one of his elder brothers. He caught smallpox as a youth and as a result suffered from a weakness in his right leg, which had to be amputated in 1768. More to the point, it meant he could not operate the foot peddle on his potter's wheel, meaning he was forced to pursue an interest in other matters, especially in designs for pottery and the development of different glazes.

His career marked a complete change in how pottery was produced. He introduced modern factory techniques and, much more than that, he introduced marketing concepts we can recognise today, from 'buy one, get one free' to illustrated trade catalogues, orders by post, free delivery and money-back guarantees. His showrooms in London gave the public a chance to see his complete range of tableware, all displayed at the same time, and travelling salesmen were employed to sell the products made in his factories. However, he was far more than a potter with brilliant marketing skills; he also had interests in the new canal system, which opened up trade throughout England, especially around Manchester. He was a significant backer of the canal that linked the rivers Mersey and Trent. He was also a major supporter of the abolitionist movement, and he churned out tens of thousands of medallions bearing the slogan, 'Am I not a man and a brother?' They became a fashion statement, and it was possibly the very first time that the public had been able to wear jewellery as part of a campaign for social change. Think CND badges, think Wedgwood.

In the early 1760s he sold a dinner service of his new creamware to Queen Charlotte and persuaded her to allow him to call it 'Queen's ware'. The public loved the durable yet elegant pottery. In 1769 he opened new factory premises known as the Etruria Works, near Stoke-on-Trent, and ensured that his workers were properly housed by building a village of workers' cottages alongside the factory. In 1773 he brought out Jasperware. This was coloured using a blend of metallic oxides, which made the moulded reliefs, which were usually white, stand out from the background, which was generally blue. This form of ornamentation was used for vases, tableware and a whole range of ornaments.

His early business success was made possible by his marriage to his wealthy third cousin, Sarah, who brought with her a dowry believed to be worth £4,000. She bore him seven children, several of whom followed him into the business. Wedgwood was a remarkable and successful businessman. He died in 1795, leaving a thriving business that was to last through a further five generations of the family.

41. SIR JOSHUA REYNOLDS LOVED PAINTING WHORES

Joshua Reynolds was one of the most influential painters of the Georgian age – and didn't he know it! A highly political animal, he despised true talent in others, lest he suffer in comparison. He churned out portraits by the hundred, offering his sitters appointments lasting just one hour. Having done the face and general pose, he would hand the canvas over to his assistant, who would then finish the portrait, especially the folds in the fabric and the hands. This was a perfectly normal type of mass production, and it earned Reynolds 80 guineas a portrait in the 1760s. He might get through as many as six sittings in a single day.

He was born near Plymouth in 1723 and spent three years in Italy as a teenager learning the 'Grand Style'. When he returned to England in 1752 he moved to London, taking rooms in St Martin's Lane before moving to a house off Leicester Square.

He mixed in all the right circles: he was friends with the leading actors, politicians and aristocrats of the period. In 1768 he was made president of the newly formed Royal Academy – something of a poisoned chalice, given the unhappy history of earlier groups consisting of artists and their easily bruised egos. He held it all together, somehow placating those who were aggrieved by the decisions of the hanging committee, and he helped foster a British style of painting, which drew crowds every year to see the Summer Exhibition.

When Allan Ramsay died in 1784, his position as Principal Painter in Ordinary to the king came up for grabs. Thomas Gainsborough was expected to be appointed, but Reynolds threatened to resign as

President of the Royal Academy unless he was chosen (not that he wanted the position, he just didn't want it to go to Gainsborough).

He delivered a series of lectures to the students of the Royal Academy between 1769 and 1790 called *Discourses on Art*, and these critiques on the works of other artists became hugely influential. Not all his students approved: the idiosyncratic William Blake, for instance, dismissed Reynolds as an idiot, which must have made for some lively tutorials!

Reynolds was somewhat deaf and often used an ear trumpet. He never married and was happy for his sister to act as his housekeeper. Intriguingly, the one social group he painted over and over again was courtesans. They were the fashionistas of the day, and he helped make them famous. Not only did those attending the Summer Exhibition get used to seeing portraits of whores hanging next to those of the queen, but when the exhibition closed they could buy copies of the paintings as mezzotints to hang on their walls at home. Celebrity status had arrived, and it helped consolidate the careers of women like Kitty Fisher, a famous courtesan who Reynolds painted on no fewer than six occasions.

He died in 1792 and was buried in St Paul's Cathedral.

42. 'Snuffy Charlotte' Helped Promote Brightly Coloured Hankies

In the eighteenth century, snuff-taking was considered positively refined – much more so than smoking or chewing tobacco. Even George III's wife, Queen Charlotte, took snuff, earning herself the nickname 'Snuffy Charlotte'. Her love of snuff was such that she had a whole room set aside at Windsor for all the different types she had, many of the jars flavoured with diverse products, from rose petals to cinnamon. Her son, the Prince Regent, was a heavy user, and snuff was also favoured by the likes of Nelson, the Duke of Wellington and Beau Brummel. Three strands had brought it to fashion prominence – the accession of Charles II (bringing habits learned in French salons to English shores); a curious naval victory over the Spanish fleet in 1702; and an edict by Beau Nash (as Master of Ceremonies at Bath) banning smoking on the premises. All led to a veritable explosion of snuff!

Snuff had been brought to the attention of the Courts of Europe by Jean Nicot (hence 'nicotine') during the reign of Queen Elizabeth I. Nicot recommended it for its 'medicinal properties'. For the next 150 years, the use of snuff in England slowly became more common. Users generally made up their own daily supply, so as to keep it fresh. Snuff-takers would have a small container like a tinderbox, designed to hold the tightly bound rolls of tobacco leaf, known as a carotte. The tobacco leaf would be ground up using a rasp or file attached to the box. The French word for the grater or rasp gave its name to the most common type of snuff, called rapé. The powder generated by the rasp was then allowed to fall through to another compartment, from where it could be removed a few grains at a time.

The naval encounter of 1702 involved the capture of a number of ships near Cadiz. They were found to be carrying a somewhat unexpected cargo: powdered snuff. A few days later, Admiral Sir George Rooke pounced on several ships off Vigo Bay and found himself the proud owner of some 50,000 pounds of premium snuff just arrived from Havana. He sailed home and off-loaded his booty in various English ports, where it became known as Vigo Premium Snuff. Suddenly, ready-powdered snuff was all the rage.

As snuff connoisseurs emerged, however, they began to want their own mix of tobacco, not just ready-milled snuff. The Prince Regent even had different mixtures for different times of the day. Being the prince, he got Fribourg and Treyer to mix it for him, none of this DIY nonsense! After his evening meal at Windsor Castle, he was known to sit down in front of no fewer than twelve jars of different snuff, before choosing his favourite for that particular occasion; one of the duties of his chief page was to ensure that stock levels were maintained.

(And the hankies – well, have you ever *seen* what happens to a white one if a snuff-taker sneezes?)

43. BANKNOTES WERE A LICENCE TO PRINT MONEY

In the second half of the eighteenth century, the Royal Mint had great difficulty minting coins because of a shortage of silver. They responded to the problem with typical arrogance: they stopped making silver coins altogether. Such coins as were already in circulation became so worn and indecipherable that it was easy for counterfeiters to pass off shiny metal blanks as the real thing. Copper coins were also in short supply, and traders had to get their own trade tokens minted. The tokens were of limited use, because they were often only accepted in the town of issue.

War with France necessitated a radical solution: the introduction of paper money, in comparatively low denomination notes, in the 1790s. Previously, people had always dealt with gold, silver and copper, i.e. the coin's intrinsic value was the same as its face value. A piece of paper with the words 'I promise to pay ...' and signed by the director of the Bank of England was not the same as having the value in your hand, and the public took some persuading that it was a good idea.

The first notes in general circulation were £20 notes issued during the Seven Years War, necessitated by a gold shortage. There were even a few issued with a face value of a thousand pounds; their high value meant that the general public was most unlikely to come across them. The first £5 notes followed in 1793, at the start of the war against the French. Even at this early stage the paper itself was hard to replicate, and the watermark gave forgers all sorts of problems. However, the notes were unpopular and, in the minds of the general public, were inextricably linked to the war with France: those darned Frenchies were behind the change, and no one liked change.

In 1797, the uncertainty of the war caused a run on gold and depleted the bank's reserves to the point where it was forced to stop paying out gold for its notes. The Restriction Period, as it was called, lasted until 1821, and during this time the Bank of England issued £1 and £2 notes.

In 1816 the Great Recoinage rectified the currency shortage by abandoning the need for silver and copper coins to contain their face value in precious metal. The £1 sovereign took the place of the former gold guinea, and the Royal Mint quickly produced good-quality coins of a 'sensible' size.

Meanwhile, the Restriction Period prompted the Irish playwright and MP Richard Brinsley Sheridan to brand the Bank of England as 'an elderly lady in the City'. The cartoonist James Gillray adapted the phrase to 'the Old Lady of Threadneedle Street', a name that has stuck ever since.

The Bank of England did not have a monopoly on printing notes, as private banks were also allowed to do so, and country banks continued to print their own until the 1844 Bank Charter Act.

44. BRISTOL BLUE WAS NOT WEST COUNTRY PORNOGRAPHY

In the eighteenth century Bristol was famous for the manufacture of glass. The city produced vast quantities of clear glass, used in windows, bottles, etc., and also a brilliantly coloured rich-blue glass used in decorative tableware. Indeed, the city gave its name to this particular type of glass – Bristol Blue – although much of the blue glassware was actually made elsewhere.

How did this come about? The underlying glassmaking skills flourished in Bristol due to a huge local demand: the fine new houses in the city and in nearby Bath all needed large quantities of glazing. Indeed, it has been estimated that over half of all glass used in England in the eighteenth century was produced in Bristol (to say nothing of the glass exported to the colonies). There was plenty of coal nearby to fire the furnaces – it was mined in many areas around Bristol – and sand, a main ingredient in glassmaking, was also readily available along the coastline of the Bristol Channel.

At some stage the manufacturing process received a huge boost with the (English) invention of the conical chimney, enabling noxious gasses from the furnaces to be drawn upwards and out into the atmosphere. The choking and often dangerous conditions in which the men worked started to improve, and the cone-shaped kilns began to appear all over the city; at one stage there may have been as many as sixty, and a commentator at the time remarked that in Bristol there were as many glassworks chimneys as church spires. There were two types of glass being produced: bottle glass and lead crystal. The latter was often taxed at a much higher rate. Lead for this more expensive glass was readily available in the Mendip Hills near Bristol.

It is at this juncture that two men appeared on the scene and transformed the city's glassmaking reputation. The first was a Bristol merchant and potter named Richard Champion. He used glassmaking technology to develop a recipe for making porcelain, which he patented. He then approached the chemist William Cookworthy, wanting a way of emulating the blue-on-white porcelain of the Far East. Cookworthy knew about cobalt oxide, known as smalt, which was being mined at the Royal Saxon Cobalt Works in Saxony. When production ceased in around 1753, Cookworthy bought the exclusive rights to all remaining smalt stocks, and over the next twenty years they were brought into England by ship to just one port – Bristol. The glassmakers of Bristol suddenly found themselves with easy access to the mineral, which they could mix with lead glass to make a beautiful, soft-blue material. Its fame was partly down to a Jewish refugee called Isaac Jacobs, who settled in Bristol from Germany and who opened a factory making blue glassware. He and his son Lazarus Jacobs greatly popularised the product. Other glassmakers in other cities had to buy the cobalt from Cookworthy in Bristol, and this helped give rise to the name 'Bristol Blue'.

45. With William Pitt It Really Was a Case of 'Like Father, Like Son'.

William Pitt, father and son, dominated the political scene for much of the eighteenth century. The father was actually only prime minister for two years and achieved most of his successes before he came to that office. His son, on the other hand, became prime minister at the ridiculously early age of twenty-four and held the post on and off for nineteen years.

The elder William Pitt was born in 1708, entering Parliament in 1735 as a dedicated opponent of Sir Robert Walpole. More than anyone else before him, he recognised the importance of public and not just parliamentary support. He was heavily critical of the foreign policy of George II and his ministers, especially in terms of the conduct of war with Spain. He realised the vital importance of our colonial interests and is often regarded as the true father of the British Empire. In Parliament he was an outstanding orator, with a withering line in sarcasm. During the premierships of both Lord Devonshire and Lord Newcastle, Pitt was effectively 'the power behind the throne', simply because he commanded such widespread public support. He was, however, generally distrusted by George II.

To Pitt the Elder must go much of the credit for the military successes in 1759, and for the strong position Britain found herself in at the end of the Seven Years War. He was frequently known as 'The Great Commoner'. He was made prime minister in 1766, but two years later left the House of Commons and became the Earl of Chatham, dying in 1778.

His precocious son became an MP at twenty-one,

and initially found himself on the same side as Charles Fox in wanting to end the war with America; they soon clashed, however, and became bitter rivals for the rest of their careers. Within a year he was made Chancellor of the Exchequer and Leader of the House, and took over the premiership in 1783 – a tenure that lasted unbroken until 1801. During his watch, the country prospered greatly. He took measures to reduce the national debt; pushed through the India Bill in 1784, limiting the powers of the East India Company; and tried (but failed) to rid Parliament of rotten borough constituencies. He led Britain to war with France in 1793 and, after the Battle of Trafalgar, was regarded as a national hero. He steered through the Act of Union with Ireland in 1800, leading to the formal union of the two kingdoms effective on 1 January 1801. However, his attempt to end discrimination against Catholics failed when the king refused to ratify his Emancipation of Catholics Bill, and, having lost the confidence of the king, he resigned in a huff. He was asked to come back three years later, but by then he was in poor health. In January 1806 he died after uttering his final words: 'Oh my country! How I love my country!' He was just forty-six years old.

46. Charles Fox Was a Politician Who Gambled, Lost a Fortune, but Won Love

Charles James Fox loved three things to excess: gambling, drinking and womanising. Of those three, gambling was his greatest love, and in the course of his life he is believed to have lost over £200,000 – a staggering sum of money, equivalent to perhaps £18 million today. Small wonder that he was bankrupted twice in the 1780s, and spent much of his subsequent life dependent upon others.

Fox's drinking bouts were legendary, and much of the antipathy towards him on the part of George III was due to the fact that the monarch held Fox responsible for leading the Prince of Wales astray. He was instrumental in assisting the prince's affair with Mary 'Perdita' Robinson, the well-known actress-courtesan, and subsequently Fox too had an affair with her. His whoring stopped rather suddenly when he fell in love with another of the prince's former mistresses, the courtesan Elizabeth Armistead. In 1785 she became Fox's mistress, but in a remarkable turn of events she tamed the wild animal in him and introduced him to a life of domesticity and true happiness. In 1795 Fox married Elizabeth, albeit in secret. She had used her own money to bail out his finances and buy a home for them in Chertsey, Surrey, where they lived in great contentment, reading and gardening. When Fox was compelled to travel to London on parliamentary business without her, his letters to Elizabeth show a deeply devoted and loving man.

George III, however, always saw Fox as the Prince Regent's tutor in debauchery and vice, and the king loathed him accordingly. The dislike was mutual, and

Fox spent much of his parliamentary career opposing what he saw as an attempt by the king to usurp the role and power of Parliament. Fox infuriated the king with his open support of the American colonies and their claim for independence, going so far as to wear the buff and blue colours of the uniforms of George Washington's army. Fox also rejoiced when the French overthrew their monarchy, although his cheers turned to tears when he heard of the subsequent execution of the French king.

It had all started with such promise. In 1768 Fox's father Henry, a prominent Whig, had bought his nineteen-year-old son a seat in Parliament, even though technically he was too young either to attend or vote. Charles and the younger William Pitt therefore entered Parliament at much the same time, but whereas Pitt went on to spend his career almost entirely at the very top, Fox spent nearly all of his career sitting on the opposition benches. His wonderful oratory, his charisma and charm, his dogged determination to defend civil liberties, to thwart the king's tyrannical aspirations and to cut Pitt down to size at every opportunity made him an immensely popular politician. No wonder he was called 'the man of the people'. He was also one of the most pilloried targets of caricaturists, especially Gillray.

47. If Priestley Had His Way We Would All Be Breathing Dephlogisticated Air

It is not easy to put Joseph Priestley into the category of 'chemist', because the majority of his 150 published works were on theological matters, and even his scientific papers were written in terms of how they affected his views about God. He must have been a precocious child, learning more than six different languages, including Latin, Hebrew, Arabic and Greek. He also learned mathematics, logic, metaphysics and natural philosophy, before deciding upon a career as a Dissenting clergyman. (This does not imply that he was a particularly quarrelsome member of the clergy, but rather that he was a committed Rational Dissenter.) One of his first major scientific works was on the properties of electricity, inspired by contact with Benjamin Franklin. He devised a number of new experiments, and repeated a number of existing ones, before publishing *The History of Electricity* in 1767.

For a comparatively short period of time (between 1773 and 1780) he worked at Bowood House, near Calne in Wiltshire. It was during this time that most of his research into gases took place. He identified no fewer than eight gases, including oxygen (which he described as a dephlogisticated air). It is fair to point out that although the discovery of oxygen is often attributed to him, both his rivals Lavoisier and Scheele came up with identical findings at much the same time. He resolutely defended the principle of phlogiston: a somewhat obscure theory based upon the flammability of substances, which was used to explain a variety of chemical processes such as combustion, calcination, smelting and respiration. Other gases identified by

Priestley included 'nitrous air' (nitric oxide); 'vapour of spirit of salt' (anhydrous hydrochloric acid); 'alkaline air' (ammonia); and 'diminished' or 'dephlogisticated nitrous air' (nitrous oxide). He isolated carbon monoxide, but without appreciating that it was a separate 'air'.

Working next to a brewery with a regular source of carbon dioxide led him to identify ways of carbonating water. He never used the discovery commercially, leaving it to men like Jacob Schweppe to develop a market for carbonated, i.e. fizzy, drinks. Jacob was a young watchmaker and a keen amateur scientist. He started a factory in Geneva in 1783, producing fizzy water. He made the ambitious claim that it had medicinal properties that could cure both indigestion and gout. Success in Geneva led him to open premises in London's Drury Lane at the end of that decade. In time, he branched out into making fizzy lemonade, and the rest is history.

By then, Priestley had rather blotted his copybook with the English authorities with his support for the French Revolution. He became known by the nickname 'Gunpowder Joe' because of his anti-monarchy views; the rioting that destroyed his home and laboratory is described elsewhere. Priestley emigrated to America with his family, determined to set up a model community on undeveloped land in Pennsylvania. The community never materialised, but he helped establish the first Unitarian chapels in the United States. He died in Pennsylvania in 1804, at the age of seventy.

48. The Poor Prayed 'Give Us Our Daily Bread' – but Many Went Without

Bread was a staple part of the diet in the Georgian era. The price of a loaf had always been a sensitive issue, and for centuries it had been controlled by the local assizes. Loaves were sold in multiples of one penny, and the assizes laid down what a penny, twopenny and threepenny loaf should weigh; this varied according to the size of the previous year's harvest and the cost of flour. Strict penalties were laid down for any baker selling underweight loaves, giving rise to the expression 'a baker's dozen' meaning thirteen, because if a baker made thirteen loaves, even if one of them were to be underweight, collectively they would still comply with the law. Individual loaves were stamped to show whether they were wheaten, made out of the best sort of flour (marked 'WH'), or the slightly less pure white ('W'). In 1757 legislation introduced a cheaper loaf known as the household loaf ('H'), which used coarser grain. In general, buyers got twice as much bread for their money in a household loaf compared with a white loaf, but the public never really liked the coarser loaf. One added problem was that unscrupulous millers added all manner of substances to pad out the milled flour – anything, as long as it was white in colour. Chalk, alum and, incredibly, oven-dried dog faeces all made their way into loaves sold to the public.

A succession of disastrous harvests occurred in the 1790s, with a particularly bad harvest in 1795 doubling the cost of flour. Food riots broke out in many parts of the country. Britain had a tradition of localised riots against rising food prices, and those in the 1790s, lasting though until 1801, followed on from other instances recorded in 1740, 1756/7, 1773 and 1782. These riots were more accurately seen as attempts to restore the status quo, protesting at mills where millers were hoarding flour in order to inflate prices, rather than to loot and destroy commercial premises. They usually had a specific object: to seize grain reserves and force its sale at the prices which previously applied.

The rate of inflation rose significantly as war with France increased the cost of foodstuffs, and Parliament decided to allow the wheat to be mixed with oats, rye and barley (all grains traditionally regarded as cattle feed and costing much less than pure wheat). The poor were outraged, but many had little choice, as the price of bread had rocketed from a penny and one farthing to threepence. Parliament decided in 1823 that within the boundaries of the City of London and within a radius of 10 miles from the centre,

> it shall be lawful for the bakers to make and sell bread made of wheat, barley, rye, oats, buck-wheat, Indian-corn, peas, beans, rice, or potatoes, or any of them, along with common salt, pure-water, eggs, milk, barm-leaven ... or other yeast, and mixed in such proportions as they shall think fit.

49. Excessive Sugar Consumption Gave Dentists a Busy Time

The increase in the consumption of sugar in the Georgian era was staggering, as shown by the fact that in 1704 the port of Liverpool imported just 760 tons of sugar, whereas a century later imports were running at 46,000 tons. Bristol had the same story, competing with Liverpool for trade in what was known as the Golden Triangle. Textiles, small arms and metal goods were exported to Africa. These goods were traded for slaves to take from Africa to the West Indies on what was called the Middle Passage, and the slaves were then traded for tobacco, cotton, rum and sugar, which would be brought back to Britain on the return leg. For the merchants, huge profits were made on each leg of the journey.

The imports spawned whole new industries, especially with sugar, which was refined, processed and sold to the public, generally in the form of conically shaped sugar 'loaves'. It could then be broken off with sugar pincers. The Georgians slathered it on their food, in their cooking and in their drinks, especially tea. Sugar was, of course, a commodity more popular with the rich than the poor, and therefore it was the rich who paid the price with appalling teeth, necessitating frequent trips to the dentist. There the rich could have 'implants' fitted – healthy teeth which would have been extracted from the gums of the poor and then wedged into the gaps left by the teeth that had become rotten and which the dentist had pulled out. Other implants were made of wood or ivory. The sugar-rich diets also caused gout, with well-known sufferers including Dr Johnson, Robert Clive and the Prince of Wales.

By 1791 there was a growing awareness that sugar consumption lay at the heart of the slave trade, and that eating sugar was encouraging something which increasing numbers of people saw as pernicious, vile and inhuman. Calls for a boycott of West Indian sugar were taken up by the general public, in a campaign which showed for the first time that consumer power could shape world events. The poet Robert Southey spoke of tea as 'the blood-sweetened beverage', and Sir William Fox urged the tea drinker 'as he sweetens his tea, let him ... say as he truly may, this lump cost the poor slave a groan, and this a bloody stroke with a cartwhip'. Caricaturists such as Gillray portrayed sugar drinkers as cannibals, and shops took to selling sugar in bowls marked 'Sugar from the East Indies' to show that it was untainted by having been produced on slave plantations. The boycott spread rapidly until, by 1794, it is estimated that over 300,000 families had joined the protest. Grocers reported that demand had fallen by a third. The boycott helped reduce consumption, and before long the plantation owners were faced with falling profits. Since slavery was driven solely by profit and greed, it meant that there was far less opposition to the trade being abolished.

50. MODERN HORSE RACING TRADITIONS STARTED WITH THE GEORGIANS

Many of the key names and traditions of modern horse racing date back to the second half of the eighteenth century. Think Jockey Club (founded in 1750); think Tattersall's (bloodstock auctioneers, founded by Richard Tattersall with headquarters off Hyde Park in 1766); think thoroughbred stud books (John Weatherby produced the first one in 1791, and it has been maintained ever since by Weatherby's, meticulously recording every thoroughbred birth in England and Ireland). In addition to these landmarks, 1776 saw the first running of the St Leger Stakes, while The Oaks was first raced in 1779 and the Epsom Derby in 1780. The 2,000 Guineas followed in 1809, with the 1,000 Guineas bringing up the rear five years after that. Both of these were held at Newmarket, which had been the traditional home of racing since early Stuart times. Up until 1753, formal races at Newmarket only took place twice a year – once in April, once in October – but in that year a second spring meeting was added. The first recorded steeple chase, i.e. a race between two church steeples, took place near Cork in Ireland in 1752, and the first recognised English National Steeplechase was held in 1830.

The period also saw the introduction of racing colours, known now as silks, in 1762. Their use was adopted by the Jockey Club with the record as follows:

For the greater conveniency of distinguishing the horses running, as also for the prevention of disputes arising from not knowing the colours worn by each rider, the underwritten gentlemen have come to the resolution and agreement of having the colours annexed to the following names, worn by their respective riders: The stewards therefore hope, in the name of the Jockey Club, that the named gentlemen will take care that the riders be provided with dresses accordingly.

Nineteen owners appended their names to the agreement: seven dukes, one marquis, four earls, one viscount, one lord, two baronets and three commoners. Originally, a black velvet huntsman's cap was the only type used by the riders, but this gave way to caps in various colours, as we know them today.

William Douglas (1725–1810), who later became known as 'Old Q' once he became the 4th Duke of Queensbury, had originally chosen white silks, but then reverted to using black and red racing colours for an astonishing fifty-seven consecutive years of racing, between 1748 and 1805. He was an infamous old roué, but a great supporter of racing and a devoted gambler. No mean amateur jockey himself, on one occasion his chosen jockey informed him that the bookmakers were offering him money to throw a race. The duke advised him to take the money, and then on the day of the race inspected his horse in the parade ring. He announced that it was such a fine horse he would ride it himself, and promptly removed his great coat to reveal his red and black silks underneath. He won the race.

51. Shoelaces Made Metal Workers Redundant

Writing on 22 January 1660, the diarist Samuel Pepys recorded, 'This day I began to put buckles on my shoes'. He was at the absolute height of fashion, and the restoration of the monarchy was accompanied by the rapid decline of the ubiquitous boot and the arrival of the humble shoe. This in turn led to the development of the coloured and often richly embroidered stocking. The finest ones were handmade out of silk by hosiers. No lady or gentleman of fashion would have been seen dead in anything other than silk, although care had to be taken to switch to black stockings if ever the Court went into mourning (which was quite often).

The actual manufacture of the leather shoe would have been carried out by a member of the Worshipful Company of Cordwainers, named after the Spanish city of Cordoba, where the very best leather (goatskin) came from. Mind you, ladies of refinement would have been far more likely to wear silk shoes indoors, saving leather for outside use. Shoes with shaped, high heels were worn by the upper classes, regardless of gender, with the heels made out of wood and positioned under the arch of the foot, rather than the actual heel. The top of the shoe was often elaborately decorated, either with embroidered silk or heavy patterned brocades, or with painted leather. Up until the Victorian era shoes were interchangeable – there was no 'left' and 'right' shoe, as both were made on the same cobblers last. Diamond-encrusted buckles were popular throughout the eighteenth century, but, if diamonds were beyond your pocket, high-quality rhinestones (which were small pieces of quartz that washed up on the banks of the River Rhine) were also used along with paste (glass).

Laces swept across the board in around 1790, driving the buckle into obscurity. Okay, they are still worn by High Court judges on Law Sunday processions, but hey, they still wear full wigs, so they don't really count as mainstream fashion arbiters!

The actual date when shoelaces are first recorded is very specific: 27 March 1790. The buckle-making industry, particularly centred in Wolverhampton, Birmingham and Walsall, collapsed almost overnight. In vain, the buckle-makers went to see the Prince of Wales at Carlton House. It was reported at the time,

> The object of their audience was to present a petition, setting forth the distressed situation of thousands of individuals in different branches of the buckle manufacture in consequence of the fashion then prevailing of wearing strings. His Royal Highness received the petitioners very graciously and, as proof of his sympathy, not only resolved to wear buckles himself but to order that his household should do the same.

A fat lot of good that did, the same source recording that

> by 1812, the whole generation of fashions, in the buckle line, was extinct: a buckle was not to be found on a female foot, nor upon any foot except that of old age.

52. Manufacturers of Tinder Boxes and Flintlocks Hated Mr Walker

The history of the friction match starts with the story of John Walker, a chemist working in Stockton-on-Tees. He had originally trained as a surgeon-doctor, but gave up the medical profession on discovering that he could not stand the sight of blood. Instead, he used his medical training to qualify as a pharmacist and wholesale druggist, opening a shop in Stockton-on-Tees in 1819. He was then thirty-eight. In 1827 he began experimenting with chemicals which would burst into flames. He used a short piece of cardboard, coated in sulphur and topped off with a mixture of sulphide of antimony, chlorate of potash and gum. Pulling the mixture through folded sandpaper ignited the cardboard. He made improvements, such as replacing the cardboard with a three-inch long wooden splint, and suddenly the financial prospects for manufacturers of tinder boxes looked very bleak indeed.

Walker initially called his invention 'friction lights', and declined to apply for a patent, but sold them as a box of fifty matches for 1s, the price to include the piece of folded sandpaper. By then Walker was calling the matches 'Congreves' in honour of the rocket pioneer Sir William Congreve. They rapidly became popular in Stockton and the surrounding towns.

Despite selling his first Congreves in April 1827, no one really gave credit to Walker for his invention. Instead, it was claimed by Samuel Jones, a Londoner who copied Walker's ideas to the letter and who launched his own 'Lucifers' in 1829. Others came up with their own ingredients for 'safety' friction matches, and suddenly fire was portable, instant and safe.

Overnight, tinder boxes, which had been churned out in their thousands, were relegated to being museum pieces. After all, who wanted to go to the trouble of trying to strike a light by knocking a flint-stone (and often their knuckles) with a metal bar called a fire-steel, when they could strike a light with a safety match? The old tinderbox would have contained at least three items – a flint, a fire-steel and a piece of tinder (typically char-cloth). The char-cloth was made by scorching a piece of material so that it was easy to ignite. An old piece of linen would be held by tongs close to the flames until it blackened. It would then be allowed to burn for a fraction of time, before being extinguished and popped into the box for future use. The box might also contain matchsticks (known as 'punks') made of deal dipped in brimstone, which would be lit from the char-cloth, and a damper (to extinguish the char-cloth after it had been used). Once the flame had been transferred from the char-cloth to the punk, it could then be transferred to a candle and, hey presto, you had fire and light. It was time-consuming and it is small wonder that the new safety match quickly caught on, and all the old paraphernalia associated with lighting fires disappeared into the history books.

53. TO BE FRANK, IT WAS NEVER AN ENTIRE NECESSITY TO HAVE AN ENVELOPE

Before the advent of the Penny Post in 1840, people rarely used envelopes because postal fees (payable by the recipient and not by the sender) were based not on weight, but on the number of sheets of paper sent – and an envelope counted as a separate sheet. People therefore omitted the envelope, and used a single piece of paper folded in three. The 'wings' would be tucked in at the back, so that the address could be written clearly on the face of the letter. Unfolding it, the writer could then fill every part of the letter, often turning it sideways to fill in the insides of the wings. Once the letter was finished, it would be sealed across the back so that the wings could not be opened up. The seal, made of wax, was known as a wafer.

These addressed letters are known as 'entires' and are now very collectible. Because the roads between neighbouring towns were frequently appalling, the entires often give directions that the letter was to be carried up to London first and then brought back to its intended destination by one of the London mail coaches. Prior to the Stamp Act of 1765, the address of the recipient was often a coffee house (there it would be collected by the addressee) or a premises described by reference to the nearest church or tavern (such as 'opposite the sign of the Blue Angel'). The 1765 Act brought in compulsory street numbering to London, although it took another decade to be universally used in the capital. In time, other cities followed suit.

The frank was a parliamentary privilege whereby Members of Parliament were entitled to free postage on constituency business. In practice, there was a widespread racket, whereby MPs sold these franks, or doled them out to friends. In 1764 Parliament tried to stop franks being counterfeited by making it a felony, punishable by up to seven years transportation, to forge the signature of an MP on the frank.

Rowland Hill published his paper 'Post Office Reform: its Importance and Practicability' right at the end of the Georgian period. Never having been inside a Post Office in his life, he was able to give a completely new opinion on the problems of delivering mail all over the country, at a uniform price. The result – the Penny Post – came in in 1840, when a staggering 9 million letters were delivered. Suddenly, people who wanted their correspondence to be private – and perhaps to enclose items with the actual letter – could do so, because the envelope shot into vogue. It seemed as if in every store clerks sat with a tin template, cutting out the shape of an open envelope onto paper and then folding and gluing the sides. The 'entire' disappeared from fashion straight away.

Post script: The first airmail letter was sent by balloon across the English Channel in January 1785, addressed to Benjamin Franklin's grandson.

54. 'CAPABILITY' BROWN DESTROYED MORE GARDENS THAN ANYONE ELSE BEFORE OR SINCE

Lancelot Brown was born in Northumberland in 1716. As a lad he became a gardener's boy at Sir William Loraine's seat at Kirkhale Hall. In 1741 he joined Lord Cobham's gardening staff at Stowe in Buckinghamshire, where he served under William Kent (one of the founders of the new English style of landscape garden). While at Stowe, Brown married a local girl (sometimes described as being Kent's daughter) and had the first of four children. He served as head gardener at Stowe before moving to London in 1751. He then purchased a small estate at Fenstanton and Hilton in 1767, acquiring the manor of Fenstanton in 1770.

The roll call of his commissions is impressive to say the least: Hampton Court, Warwick Castle, Blenheim Palace, Bowood House, Longleat, Chatsworth and, to a lesser extent, Kew Gardens, to name but a few of the 170 gardens he helped design. His nickname came from his invariable assertion to landowners that their land had 'capabilities' for improvements to the landscape. He called himself a 'place maker', rather than a landscape gardener.

His style was as far removed from the earlier formal knot gardens and planted-up flower beds as it was possible to get. Out went the parterres, statues, canals, fountains, formal topiary and stately avenues, which had hallmarked the seventeenth century. For Brown, emulating nature was the name of the game, with rolling hills, meandering streams, serpentine-shaped lakes with overhanging trees and perfect vistas at every turn.

Capability Brown died on 6 February 1783, in London, leaving behind a legacy unparalleled in the history of English gardening. Indeed, one of the criticisms made against Brown was that he had destroyed so much of what had gone before. The architect Sir William Chambers complained that Brown's grounds 'differ very little from common fields, so closely is nature copied in most of them'. Another author commented that he wanted to 'see heaven before it was "improved"' and therefore hoped to die before Brown. His works destroyed the three greatest Baroque gardens in England: Longleat House in 1757 and Chatsworth and Blenheim in 1760. In its place he brought a parkland style which became so popular that there can hardly be a stately home in the country which doesn't show Brown's influence to some degree.

Brown was followed by Humphry Repton, who became famous for his 'little red books' – over 400 of them – each containing a detailed essay on the particular country estate, with recommendations for improvements linked to 'before and after' sketches showing different vistas and perspectives. Clients loved the way they could visualise the schemes by looking at the watercolours Repton produced to illustrate his proposals. Unlike Brown, who saw the whole project through from start to finish, from design right through to completion of all works, Repton designed his gardens and then left it to others to implement the ideas. He was the first to use the term 'landscape gardener' and died in 1818.

55. 'GET OFF MY LAND!' – THE ENCLOSURE ACTS DROVE THE RURAL POOR INTO TOWNS

There was nothing new about landowners getting permission to fence off what had previously been common land. This had been going on for five centuries, but on nothing like the scale which occurred after 1750. The result drove tens of thousands off the land and into the towns. On the one hand it caused poverty among rural communities, and on the other it led to migration into urban communities, and hence provided the labour force which made the Industrial Revolution possible.

Communities that had managed for centuries were broken up as the open field system (historically used for gleaning, growing a few subsistence crops, small-scale grazing of cattle and rearing geese and the like) was swallowed up. Ancient rights to cut peat, collect hay or firewood or forage for berries disappeared. With it went a way of life for the independent, landless poor. The advantage to the landowner doing the fencing was higher productivity resulting from larger-scale operations. More mechanisation, more economies of scale, higher crop yields and the chance to charge higher rents to tenants were all attractive features to those who wanted to fence off the common land. It has to be said, Parliament was made up of landowners, so little wonder that MPs encouraged the 'improvements' which resulted from enclosure, with little thought for the consequences.

Before enclosing common land, be it open field or 'waste', the landowner first had to obtain an Act of Parliament. Land had to be surveyed and a scheme agreed with the commissioner appointed under the

Act to compensate those being dispossessed. This compensation might be monetary or consist of the offer of alternative land, often some distance away or possibly of inferior quality. The landowner was then free to fence off the land and to treat anyone coming on to it as a trespasser.

A trickle of Tudor and Stuart enclosure cases developed into a Georgian flood. Hundreds of Enclosure Acts were passed (or, as they were called at the time, Inclosure Acts) so that by the nineteenth century the vast majority of lowland common land had been fenced off, leaving mainly the less-productive, hilly areas and a few village greens. Some 4,000 Acts were passed between 1760 and 1870, affecting some 7 million acres.

Fencing the land led to improvements in land drainage, inspired by the experiments of Joseph Elkington, who lived between 1739 and 1806. He helped drain boggy ground throughout the countryside, enabling useful crops to be grown on land which previously had no agricultural value. In time, growing more winter feedstuffs meant that livestock could be fed through the winter, instead of being killed and the meat salted down. Productivity also increased thanks to the pioneering methods of men like Robert Bakewell, who experimented with selective breeding. His breeding programmes with sheep and cattle led to far greater meat yields than had ever been thought possible.

56. Not All of His Inventions Involved Hot Air – James Watt Also Invented a Portable Copier

Watt, famous for his invention of the steam condenser and for his steam engines made in conjunction with Matthew Boulton, has one other claim to fame: the invention of the desktop letter copier. The steam engines may have powered the Industrial Revolution, but his copier remained in use in offices up and down the land for over 100 years.

Watt was born in Scotland in 1736 and had at one stage trained as an instrument maker. Later, on those endlessly long journeys from his offices in Birmingham to oversee his modifications to the old Newcomen steam engines in Cornwall, he would write his letters – and bemoan the fact that he was obliged to write each one out twice if he wanted to keep a copy. In 1779 he began experimenting with a device that used multiple pens linked by rods, but the machine was cumbersome and getting the pressure right on all the pens at the same time was difficult, so James looked at the problem from a different perspective. Having experimented with different (unsized) papers and various inks mixed with gum Arabic, he came up with the idea of pressing the original page against a thin tissue paper, so that surplus ink could be offset onto the duplicate sheet. Turn the tissue paper over and the writing would be the correct way round. The invention had the advantage that it produced an exact copy and could be used for drawings just as effectively as lettering.

Various refinements were made to the idea before Watt registered his patent in 1780. Moistening the tissue paper was central to the scheme, and the rollers or screw press (he experimented with both) had to apply an even pressure. The ink had to be slow drying, but he ended up with a system which could copy an unblotted page of inked paper for several hours after it had been written.

Watt was already in partnership with Matthew Boulton, so it was natural that he should again go into partnership with the industrialist to develop the copier. The business was known as James Watt & Co., and by the end of the first full year's trading 630 copiers had been sold. For the next 100 years the invention (and its numerous imitations) was an invaluable office machine.

Watt is best remembered for his work with steam and, ironically, with horses. He calculated the power of his engines in terms of horsepower, and then charged extra for those engines on the basis of how many horses would no longer be needed to be fed and looked after over a ten-year period. Mine owners had little choice but to comply with this surcharge, since the Watt monopoly on the condensing cylinder was extended in 1775 and did not run out until 1800. Watt died in 1819 at his home near Birmingham, at the age of eighty-three, indelibly associated with the Industrial Revolution.

57. Paul May Have Been Revered by One George (Washington), but Never by Another (George III)

The War of American Independence started in 1775 and ended with the Treaty of Paris in 1783, although fighting had petered out two years earlier after the surrender of the British at Yorktown. Britain had found that its resources were spread too thinly, especially once the French, Dutch and Spanish had joined in the conflict. The expense was crippling to Britain's economy, with the war costing some £80 million, leaving the country with a national debt of £250 million. The Navy was decimated by the desertion of over 40,000 sailors, coupled with the death of another 20,000, of whom nearly 1,850 perished from starvation and disease.

The background to the war is well documented, with the colonial demands for 'no taxation without representation' being put forward in response to British attempts to impose levels of taxation without reference to the colonies. The American Declaration of Independence in 1776 claimed independence for the thirteen colonies, and it was followed by desultory fighting, a few inconclusive victories for the British (Bunkers Hill near Boston, the Battle of Long Island, Washington and the capture of New York) and a few notable successes for the army of General Washington (Trenton, Princeton and Saratoga and Yorktown).

Many legends grew up around the conflict, few more romantic than the story of Paul Revere's midnight ride on 18 April 1775. Revere was a Boston silversmith, who also tried his hand at dentistry (the false teeth he made for George Washington still exist) and eventually became one of the most famous patriots in the war against Britain. American forces had got wind of the British plan to march on Concord and Lexington to seize weapons stored there and, if possible, to capture Samuel Adams and John Hancock, two of the rebel leaders. Revere determined to get through to Concord and Lexington to warn the residents of what lay in store for them. Rowing across the Charles River under the noses of the British fleet, he rode along roads patrolled by enemy forces, reportedly shouting out the warning 'the British are coming' (but more probably 'the Regulars are coming') to all the householders along the way. Others took up the cry, and by the end of the night as many as forty riders were spreading the news of the imminent attack. Revere reached Lexington at midnight and raced on to Concord, but was stopped at gunpoint by a British patrol and taken prisoner. His companion, Dr Prescott, leaped a wall and escaped capture, making it to Concord.

Revere was released in time to hear the opening shots of the war at Lexington Green. He rejoined his artillery troop and was involved in the disastrous Penobscot Expedition, where the American forces were routed. Revere was court-martialled and was exonerated but took no further part in the conflict. It took until 1861 for Paul Revere to achieve immortality, with the publication of Longfellow's poem 'The Midnight Ride'.

58. Mr Churchman Made Exceedingly Good Chocolate

Chocolate had long been famed for its medicinal properties, rather than as a piece of confectionary. Cocoa beans had originally been brought back by the Spanish from South America, where chocolate was a favourite (cold) drink of the native Aztecs. They regarded it as a potent aphrodisiac and knocked it back by the gallon. The Spanish experimented by adding a variety of spices, such as sugar, cinnamon, cloves, vanilla and pepper, to make the bitter taste more palatable to European tastes. When they started making it with hot water the drink was swiftly adopted as the preferred drink of the Spanish Court – indeed, a royal decree limited consumption to the nobility and members of the royal family.

In England, Sir Hans Sloane (he of Sloane Square fame) came up with the idea of mixing the crushed beans with hot milk. The drink rapidly became popular, especially among the aristocrats and wealthy merchants who frequented London's Coffee Houses.

Chocolate was not easy to produce from the beans of the cocoa tree, and various attempts were made to crush them mechanically until Walter Churchman came up with a hydraulic grinding press, which he patented in 1720. He, along with so many of the early chocolate manufacturers, was a Quaker, just like Joseph Terry of York, John Cadbury of Birmingham and Mary Tuke, also from York, who later sold her business to another Quaker by the name of Rowntree. Churchman was a pharmacist, whose religious beliefs prevented him from qualifying as a doctor. To be a doctor you needed to be a graduate, but Quakers were barred from matriculating, and presumably for him, being a pharmacist was the next best thing. From his premises in Bristol he offered superfine chocolate for sale at 6s a pound. Walter died, leaving his son Charles, a lawyer, to carry on the business.

By then, Joseph Fry, another Quaker pharmacist, had also started selling chocolate, as borne out by advertisements for the product dating back to the mid-1700s. When Charles Churchman died in 1761, he left the chocolate patent rights and the business to his executor, James Vaughan. James went into partnership with Joseph Fry to expand the Churchman business. Within three years the company, known as Fry, Vaughan & Co., had agents in over fifty cities throughout the country, along with large storage premises in London.

Joseph Fry died in 1787 and the business was taken over by his widow, Anna. She in turn passed control to her son, and he was responsible for the installation, in 1795, of a Boulton & Watt steam engine to help in the manufacturing process. Before long, the Fry company was producing nearly half of all chocolate manufactured in this country. By 1825 the majority of cocoa beans were being bought by the Royal Navy, which considered it an ideal drink for sailors. Those on watch duty in the Atlantic Ocean and the Baltic Sea called the cold wind from the north-west 'the chocolate gale'.

59. Australia Was Never a Holiday Destination

Given that Parliament exclusively represented the interests of its own members, all of whom were landowners, it is little wonder that so many of the criminal offences that carried the most severe penalties were those which affected property rights. Parliament looked after its own. There were, therefore, well over 200 offences on the Statute Book carrying the death penalty by 1770, the vast majority of them relating to what we would now see as variations of theft. People could be sent to the gallows for poaching, highway robbery, burglary and even just stealing a few shillings. In many cases the death sentence was commuted to a sentence of transportation. This proved popular with the authorities: it not only punished the offender, but removed him (or her) from society so as to lessen the risk and consequences of reoffending.

The Transportation Act of 1718 allowed judges to order transportation to the American colonies for a term of up to seven years. That worked well until 1776, when war with America suspended this harsh penalty. Before that time some 60,000 prisoners had been transported. Afterwards, prisoners were incarcerated in rotting hulks in the River Thames instead. In each of these floating prisons up to 300 men would be held in cramped quarters and appalling conditions. Typhoid and cholera were endemic, causing the deaths of nearly a third of all 6,000 convicts held on hulks between 1776 and 1795. Feeding the prisoners in these hulks cost money: money which could be saved if the convicts were simply shipped out of the country. In 1787, transportation resumed, this time to Australia.

What became known as the First Fleet, with 775 convicts crammed into six transport ships, reached Botany Bay in New South Wales on 20 January 1788, after a voyage of eight months. Convicts and crew alike were desperately short of food, a position made even worse when the disastrous Second Fleet arrived in 1790, carrying more sick and dying passengers but no supplies.

Convicts sentenced to transportation were either given fixed-term or lifetime sentences. At the end of the fixed term, convicts were free to return to Britain as long as they could find the fare. For many this was impracticable, and they stayed on as free men. Those sentenced to life and who had served a substantial term of years could apply for a ticket to leave, enabling them to marry, raise a family and take part in colonial life.

For forty years, huge numbers of convicted felons, around one-fifth of them women, were sent into exile, particularly via what was then Port Jackson (now Sydney). Between 1803 and 1853 Tasmania was used as a penal colony, with thousands arriving to harsh and brutal conditions via Hobart. Transportation to New South Wales stopped in 1840, by which time some 150,000 convicts had been brought into the colony, some of them children as young as nine. Eventually, penal servitude replaced transportation in 1857.

60. Smugglers Loved War with France

The title 'HM Customs and Excise' betrays the fact that two completely different taxes are being collected. Customs are levied on the value of imported goods entering the country. Since the Middle Ages this levy was passed to the Crown, and in 1688 an Act was passed to streamline the collection and ensure that funds passed into the hands of the government and not the king personally. Excise, on the other hand, was a tax on domestic consumption, and at the time of the Civil War it covered a variety of goods, in particular products used in making luxury drinks such as chocolate, tea and coffee. Beer, cider and spirits were also subject to Excise Duty, and after 1688 the tax net was widened to include essentials such as salt, leather and soap. Within fifty years the level of duty on these products had increased dramatically, especially at times when Britain was at war, because excise duties were seen as a convenient way of raising revenue to pay for the fighting.

War with France also had the effect of reducing the availability of goods being imported legally from that country. Demand for French wine and brandy led to an explosion in smuggling. Along the South Coast, and particularly in Cornwall and the Scilly Isles, whole communities became economically dependent upon smuggling. The value of cargoes of illegally imported goods is difficult to assess, but reports suggested that, at times, well over half of all tea imported into the country was smuggled in, thereby avoiding tax. During the Seven Years War and the Napoleonic Wars, the smuggling of cognac and French wines took place on a truly industrial scale.

In the French ports such as Calais, Boulogne, Dunkirk, Roscoff and Le Havre, the smugglers' agents grew wealthy, fulfilling orders and loading the goods to be smuggled into easy-to-carry containers on the quayside. Ships would load up, cross the Channel and usually unload their cargoes at night, out of sight of the Excise Men, and there was never a shortage of farm labourers and fishermen willing to lug the barrels and other containers up the cliffs and into ready-prepared caves, lock-ups and secret tunnels. The profit margins were impressive, with tea being available on the Continent at a few pence per pound weight and retailing in this country at 15s for the same quantity. Cognac, smuggled in in small barrels at a cost of £1 per barrel in France, would retail at over four times that amount in England (rather more than quadruple the price when you consider that retailers would first water down the brandy, because the imported product was so ridiculously strong). Smugglers had their own banks to finance their operations. Their cutters could outrun the ships used by Customs and Excise, and until the end of the Napoleonic Wars the smugglers had the upper hand. Only with the introduction of free-trade areas in the 1840s did smuggling cease to be commercially viable.

61. COUNTERFEITING COINS WAS DEADLY

On 27 October 1779 a woman emerged from Newgate prison, attached to a hurdle dragged behind a cart. Thus, she was taken to Tyburn (near the site of today's Marble Arch). Once there, she had a rope attached to her neck and kindling wood and faggots were stacked around her. Just before the flaming torch was put to the wood, the executioner pulled on the rope, thus strangling the poor woman before the flames consumed her body. Her name was Isabella Condon.

Being burnt at the stake was a penalty applied to petty treason (e.g. if a woman murdered her husband) as well as high treason (a term which included counterfeiting coinage). Oddly, a man might only be hanged for the offence of counterfeiting, whereas his female counterpart suffered the gruesome and ghastly fate of being publicly burned alive. Of course, if she was lucky she would never feel the flames, because the executioner usually garrotted the woman before the fire took hold, but on at least one occasion in the eighteenth century the executioner let go of the rope while lighting the faggots, and was himself beaten back by the flames. He was therefore unable to retrieve the rope in order to strangle the poor woman, who died hideously and extremely slowly.

As a reminder of the cruel barbarism of 'justice' just two centuries ago, it is worth remembering that Isabella's crime was forging a single shilling, and she was caught red-handed, with the classic equipment of a counterfeiters' workshop in her possession: a saucer with wet sand, a few genuine coins, a file, a bit of sandpaper, a cork, some 'black stuff' and a pair of tweezers. There was a melting pot and an iron flask, together with a phial of 'aqua fortis' (nitric acid), a vessel for pouring the metal in the mould, a scale and white arsenic. Her claim that the paraphernalia belonged to a friend who had just left the room cut no ice, perhaps because the coins were still in the folds of her apron.

Burning remained the punishment for female forgers until 1790 – the last woman to be punished in this barbaric way was Catherine Murphy (also known as Christian Bowman), who was put to death on Wednesday 18 March 1789. *The Times* led a campaign to change the law, which was brought in originally because the equivalent punishment for men was to be hanged, drawn and quartered: this would not have been appropriate for a woman, since it would have involved public nudity. As *The Times* put it (24 June 1788), 'Must not mankind laugh at our long speeches against African slavery ... [when] ... we roast a female fellow creature alive, for putting a pennyworth of quicksilver on a halfpennyworth of brass.'

As it happened, one Thomas Condon, husband of the late Isabella, was himself hanged a few years later for counterfeiting coins. So much for the death penalty being a deterrent!

62. Global Cooling, Not Warming, Was a Hot Topic

Nowadays the emphasis is on global warming, but it is worth remembering that there have always been climate cycles, and the Georgian era was a time of global cooling. The Thames froze over in 1716, 1739/40, 1789 and 1814. Cue frost fairs – impromptu festivals which were held on the ice, with tented villages springing up, fires being lit for roasting oxen and printing presses set up to produce souvenirs. There was ice skating, games and dances and vendors selling food and drink. There were inevitable problems when the thaw set in, with many instances of people being drowned as a result of falling through the ice. Some of the fairs lasted for weeks, but the final one, in 1814, lasted a mere five days.

Crowds flocked to the final fair, unaware that the conditions were never likely to be repeated. The old London Bridge, with its nineteen arches and irregular narrow gaps that dramatically slowed down the River Thames, was demolished two decades later. In its place, Rennie's new bridge, with just five stone supports, was opened in 1831, and the waters flowed more evenly. Later, the Embankment was constructed, funnelling the river so that it flowed more rapidly, and the era of the Frost Fair was over, never to be repeated. These structural changes coincided with the end of the mini 'ice age', which had lasted between 1770 and 1820. During that time it was perfectly normal for snow to lie on the ground for weeks on end. Travel could be severely handicapped as snow funnelled between the high hedges that lined the roads – and of course, snow could only be cleared by way of a man and a shovel, so whole communities could be cut off for days on end.

Between 1770 and 1820, summers were cooler and winters colder than average. There was one year which stood out from all the others – 1773/4. Over in Iceland, the Laki volcano exploded on 8 June 1773, not from its top, but from a number of fissures on its side. A volcanic fountain shot 1,400 metres into the sky, with poisonous gases being propelled into the atmosphere for months. Fluorine gas fell to the land as hydrofluoric acid, killing half the cattle and three-quarters of the sheep in Iceland and leading to widespread starvation. The cloud of noxious gas reached Europe by 22 June, and by the last week of June was affecting farm labourers throughout Britain. Crops withered, livestock died and lung injuries killed some tens of thousands of people. The cloud first trapped in the heat and then, when the sweltering summer finished, absorbed what warmth was left, causing one of the coldest winters on record to follow. In all, the volcano is believed to have caused 6 million deaths worldwide and spread famine and economic hardship to many parts of Europe. Indeed, because of the food shortages it caused, it is credited as being a contributory factor that led to the French Revolution.

63. Jethro Tull Never Played the Flute

Jethro Tull was an unusual character: he was born into a family of landowning gentry in Berkshire, in March 1674. He studied law at Gray's Inn and qualified as a barrister in 1699. He embarked on a cut-down version of the Grand Tour (it only lasted four months, instead of the more usual two years) and returned having had a glimpse of continental farming practices, especially in viticulture. He had seemed destined for a career in politics, but he suffered from a lung condition that caused him breathing difficulties and he took over the family farm instead, possibly because an outdoor life was considered beneficial to his health.

In 1710, Jethro and his family moved to Prosperous Farm near Hungerford. He was an unlikely farmer. Farmers needed to have patience; the one thing Tull was not, was patient, and he hated waste. He hated paying his men to broadcast seeds – i.e., scattering them by hand into ploughed furrows – when this was totally hit and miss. He berated the labourers for being incompetent because their wastage cost him his profits. He instructed his workmen to sow the seed at very specific densities and depths. They either refused or were unable to achieve his targets, and Tull set about experimenting with a mechanical seed drill of his own design. His machine had a revolving cylinder, fed with seed from a hopper and funnel. The seed was fed straight into a channel, which was dug by a plough attached to the front of the machine and then filled in by a harrow at the rear. Tull decided that the contraption was best suited to being pulled by horse, rather than oxen.

His original idea for the seed drill had not caught

on, and Tull modified the design by coming up with a way of pulverising the earth between the rows. This had the effect of killing weeds that might otherwise have competed with the growing seeds. He was able to demonstrate that he could grow crops year after year without the need for manure and without needing to leave the land fallow.

He also worked on a mechanical hoe and made modifications to the traditional plough, which not only tilled the soil but cut off the weeds and left them on the surface of the soil where the natural nutrients could be recycled. Mind you, he was a product of his age – brought up to believe that the roots of plants had tiny mouths which could eat the goodness in the earth. His science may have been a bit flaky, but his machines were a huge advance.

In 1731 he published his ideas as *The Horse Hoeing Husbandry*, but his methods were ridiculed by others. He was attacked in agricultural periodicals and accused of plagiarising. The controversy over his invention was to last for another century, but he was eventually vindicated and in many ways can be regarded as the forerunner of modern farming. He died in 1741.

64. Jane Austen Remained Anonymous Throughout Her Lifetime

It is a truth universally acknowledged that although Jane Austen published four novels during her lifetime, they were all published anonymously. Each book was described as having been written 'by a lady'. While she was alive she received a certain amount of critical acclaim, from writers such as Sir Walter Scott, but derived very little financial return from her writings, and certainly not enough to lift her from a life of considerably straightened circumstances. Jane, like most of her heroines, was faced with the unenviable choice of remaining single and poor, or marrying and losing all independence. Unlike her heroines, who generally waited until love prevailed and all parties got their due rewards, Jane turned her back on the one proposal of marriage she did receive and paid the price by never getting to live happily ever after.

She had been born just before Christmas in 1775 to an impecunious rector and his wife at Steventon in Hampshire. Theirs was a close-knit family; Jane had an elder sister, Cassandra (to whom she wrote most of her surviving letters), and six brothers, including Henry, who later became her literary agent. An elder brother, Edward, was adopted by a cousin, who had no child of his own and wanted a male heir. Edward eventually changed his legal surname to Knight and inherited his adoptive family's estates, enabling him to offer Chawton House to his mother and sisters. Prior to that, the family had spent nine years living at various addresses in Bath and Southampton. It was during this time that Jane visited friends in Basingstoke and got engaged (briefly) to a family friend by the curious name of Harris Bigg-Wither. Her suitor, who stuttered and had very little personality, was heir to an estate which would have enabled Jane and her family to live comfortably. A single night of reflection persuaded Jane that she did not want to be Mrs Bigg-Wither, and she broke off the engagement in the morning. Jane's father died in 1805, making her financial position even more precarious.

Both *Sense and Sensibility* (published in 1811) and *Pride and Prejudice* (published two years later) had their origins in works written at least fifteen years previously, when Jane was only just out of her teens. *Sense and Sensibility* had started life as *Elinor and Marianne*, and went through various redrafts before it emerged in its present form. Christmas 1795 was an important time for Jane, as it was then that she is believed to have met and fallen in love with a young Irish barrister called Tom Lefroy. Marriage was a financial impossibility, but the doomed relationship may well have been reflected in *Pride and Prejudice*, which Jane started writing in 1796 under the title *First Impressions*.

Emma was her last work to be published in her lifetime. *Northanger Abbey* and *Persuasion* were issued posthumously, with a preface by her brother Henry, which for the first time identified Jane as the author.

65. KETCHUP WAS NEVER RED

Etymologists argue whether the word ketchup has Chinese or Malay origins. Certainly it came to Britain with various spelling variants: Jonathan Swift was describing it as 'catsup' back in 1730. Katchup, catchup and kitchup were alternative spellings to a product which quickly became phenomenally popular throughout the English-speaking world. It had its origins in the Far East, and came to Britain as trade opened up in the 1690s. Its popularity took off as part of the vogue for 'all things Chinese' in the second half of the eighteenth century. As the import of porcelain, lacquerware and tea expanded, so it brought merchants into contact with Chinese, Malay, Vietnamese and Indonesian customs – places where a fishy, salty flavour had been developed over many centuries.

We wouldn't actually recognise Georgian ketchup. We think now of a thick, gloopy, red sauce made from tomatoes, but to the Georgians it originally meant a dark, brackish liquid infused with fermented fish extracts and, later, a type of runny chutney made from items such as fermented walnuts or mushrooms. The tomato didn't make an appearance in ketchup before 1800, and sugar really only became an ingredient fifty years after that. One (delicious?) recipe from 1736 involved boiling down 'two quarts of strong stale beer and half a pound of anchovies' and then letting it ferment. Salt and fermentation were key – and throwing in a strong smell of old fish was definitely to be encouraged!

Another ingredient used to try and imitate the original fishy flavour was the pickled walnut, but making the stuff was time-consuming, with one recipe requiring the cook to stir the mixture for eight days.

No nipping down to the supermarket and picking a bottle off the top shelf for Regency cooks! In time, the tomato began to infiltrate. It is mentioned in a recipe in 1801, and early references to it use the delightful name of 'love apple'. The sauce got sweeter and sweeter and more viscous, ending up as the modern gloop so beloved of chip eaters everywhere. The Georgians would have hated it!

Mustard was another Georgian favourite. The English manufacture of mustard had long been centred in Tewkesbury, where whole mustard seeds and stalks were crushed with a pestle and mortar, giving a rough condiment that was not especially hot to the taste. Then along came a Mrs Clements, from Durham. She treated the mustard to the full works: the mustard seeds were separated from the stems and finely milled, and the resulting fine powder contained all the heat and flavour you could possibly wish for. The story goes that on 10 June 1720, she trotted off to see her neighbours and to flog them a jar or two of her 'new improved' mustard. Word spread and before long she headed for London and introduced King George I to the delights of her condiment. Royal admirers were quick to emulate the king's good taste, and her success was assured.

66. PHILIP ASTLEY NEVER RAN AWAY TO JOIN THE CIRCUS

Philip Astley couldn't join the circus – until he created it. As a boy, he grew up in Newcastle-under-Lyme, helping out in his father's woodworking shop. His ambition was to work with horses, and at the age of seventeen he walked out on his family after a row and joined the 15th Hussars. He became a heroic figure in the Seven Years War, capturing the French flag at the Battle of Emsdorf and personally rescuing the Duke of Brunswick after the duke had fallen injured behind enemy lines. Astley charged through the lines, picked the duke up and carried him to safety. He became a typical sergeant major, with his loud, booming voice and imposing physique (he was 6-foot tall and had a girth like an oak tree). He was a brilliant horseman – the horse whisperer of his age – and when he was discharged from the Army he headed for London, determined to make a living giving riding lessons and demonstrating his equestrian skills.

He would give lessons in the morning and in the afternoon he and his pupils would put on 'a bit of a show'. The public soon flocked to watch the performance, and a bucket would be passed around for a collection. Astley expanded the show by adding a musical accompaniment. He acquired premises in Lambeth, near Westminster Bridge, and built a galleried pavilion from which onlookers could see him demonstrate his extraordinary equestrian skills in a circular arena with a diameter of 42 feet. This is still the standard size of the circus ring today.

He added speciality acts, such as jugglers, acrobats, slack wire dancers and clowns. He introduced clowning on horseback – and the public loved it. He also developed the role of the ringmaster, standing in the centre of the ring, resplendent in his red and gold uniform, cracking the whip and loudly announcing the forthcoming spectacle. He featured other domesticated animals (dogs, monkeys and even pigs) but not wild animals; horses remained central to his acts for his entire life. He went on tour in Britain and in Europe, opening some nineteen permanent sites for his circus – he actually didn't use the word, instead calling them 'amphitheatres'.

He brought in the crowds wherever he went. Here was a man who could have taught Richard Branson a thing or two about self-publicity! He was constantly in the news, and became a favourite of both the British and French royal families, frequently entertaining Marie Antoinette and her family at Versailles and in Paris. Fire was his constant enemy and he suffered from various disastrous conflagrations, but each time he would rebuild and open in time for the next season. Other copycats developed his ideas, opening circus premises throughout Europe, America and beyond. As such, Astley can fairly be claimed not only to have been the father of the modern circus, but also a pivotal figure in the history of popular entertainment. He died in Paris in 1814.

67. One Man Links Both 'Rule, Britannia!' and 'God Save the King'

Thomas Arne was born in 1710 and died in 1778, and in his lifetime was one of the country's leading music composers for the theatre. The first published version of 'God Save the King!' appeared in 1744. It became a popular patriotic song the following year, coinciding with the Jacobite Rebellion. A version of the song appears in *The Gentleman's Magazine* of 1745, where it was referred to as, 'God save our lord the king. A new song set for two voices,' and there are records that it was being performed at Covent Garden theatre after each performance.

The actual phrase 'God save the king' is much older than the song. It appears several times in the King James Bible, and it is likely that it was previously used as a watchword in the English navy, where the call of, 'God save the king!' was met by the response, 'Long to reign over us.'

The fact that the song has become a national anthem (for Great Britain, not for England, which does not have one) appears to have been a matter of custom, not law. No Act of Parliament or Royal Proclamation directed it to be played, but in practice the entire anthem is played as a salute to the reigning sovereign (and consort). Other 'lesser' royals, such as the Prince of Wales, only have to endure the first six bars of the dreadful dirge. From time to time there are calls to introduce an English anthem (just as the Welsh and the Scots have theirs), so who knows, maybe we will end up with Elgar's 'Land of Hope and Glory' for the English and we can relegate 'God Save the King' solely to British occasions.

Arne's other claim to fame is 'Rule, Britannia!' In 1740, James Thomson, a Scottish poet, wrote the words as part of a masque called *Alfred*. The masque, involving music and dance, was ostensibly about Alfred the Great, but was intended to identify the heroic figure of Alfred with Frederick, Prince of Wales. Alfred had long been regarded as the father of the English navy, and Frederick was keen to be associated with him at a time when the British fleet had been having some notable successes in the course of the War of Jenkins Ear. Cue much patriotism, and a stirring anthem was just what the audience wanted! It was performed to Arne's music to commemorate the accession of George II. The first performance was at Cliveden in front of the Prince of Wales, in August 1740. Interestingly, it was written at a time when Britain did *not* rule the waves. Indeed, the correct punctuation of the title is 'Rule, Britannia! Britannia, rule the waves!' – in other words, it was an exhortation to go out and rule. Later refinements in the Victorian era changed it to a simple statement of fact: 'Britannia *rules* the waves!'

68. CARLTON HOUSE WAS A PALACE FIT FOR A PRINCE, BUT NOT FOR A KING

Carlton House was originally a rambling home facing onto Pall Mall, with gardens stretching back to St James's Park. It was bought in 1732 by Frederick, Prince of Wales, and he brought in William Kent to design the gardens. When the prince died, his widow remained in occupation, and she extended the accommodation. In 1783, possession was granted to her grandson George, Prince of Wales. With it went an allowance of £60,000, intended to enable the prince to equip it in a manner appropriate to the eldest son of George III. The architect Henry Holland was brought in to supervise the conversion of this princely abode into an opulent palace, using a French-inspired, neo-classical style. State apartments were added along one frontage, a portico of Corinthian columns adorned the entrance way and no expense was spared in furnishing the entire property in the most ornate and elaborate manner. Craftsmen from France were engaged in the most extravagant detailing – everything was on a grand scale. Statues, sculptures, paintings and *objets de vertu* were acquired by the hundred. The cost overruns were horrendous: work had to be halted when the debts of the prince amounted to over £250,000. He had to go and beg his father for more money – not easy at a time when their relations were severely strained because of the prince's purported marriage to Mrs Fitzherbert without the king's approval.

A further allowance of £60,000 was granted, and most of the building work was completed by 1796. For a quarter of a century it was used by the prince as his main London residence, but further works were continually being carried out. The prince parted company with Henry Holland in 1802, but Thomas Hopper took his place to add on a gothic conservatory. More chinoiserie and pieces of gothic furniture were purchased. Finally, John Nash was appointed in 1813. He oversaw completion of earlier designs and put in a gothic dining room. No sooner was it all finished than the Prince Regent became king, following the death of his father in 1820. As George IV, the new king felt that Carlton House was really not appropriate to his needs. A monarch should have something altogether larger and grander, to match his status. In 1826 the entire edifice was pulled down, stone by stone, and replaced with two grand terraces of white-stuccoed houses (now Carlton House Terrace). In its place, the king upgraded Buckingham House (for years the Queen's House), making it into the suitably regal Buckingham Palace (see later). Many of the architectural features were salvaged and much of the furniture was moved to other palaces. The collection of Old Masters – paintings by Rembrandt, Rubens and Van Dyke – together with works by artists such as Reynolds, Gainsborough and Stubbs, helped form the basis of today's Royal Collection, and established the reputation of the prince as a patron of the arts.

69. POPE JOAN WAS EXTREMELY POPULAR

The eighteenth century saw an explosion in the number of different types of card game available for people to play – especially for money. Faro was one which was extremely popular, where players bet on the next card to be turned upwards, but the game fell in to disrepute because of the ease with which unscrupulous players could manipulate a crooked deck of cards. Quadrille was a game played with a forty-card pack and was mentioned in Jane Austen's *Pride and Prejudice* as a game played by Lady Catherine de Bourgh. Speculation was another game played for money (Jane Austen mentions it in *Mansfield Park*). Whist grew out of games played in London's coffee houses, and Edmund Hoyle became famous as a tutor in the rules of the game, leading to the publication of his *A Short Treatise on the Game of Whist* in 1742. Anyone wanting to play on their own could try Patience, otherwise known as Solitaire, which came into vogue in the 1780s. One of the most popular card games of the Georgian era, however, went by the odd name of Pope Joan.

So, who, what and why Pope Joan? Apparently stories started circulating in the 1300s to the effect that some 400 years earlier there had been a female pontiff, who lived her life disguised as a man. Her cover was blown when she very publicly gave birth to a child while crossing the Via Sacra between the Coliseum and St Clement's Church in Rome. Pope John VIII (as she was known) was apparently deposed (or is that de-poped?) and a lovely story suggests that subsequent pontiffs had to undergo a rather intimate examination by a selected cardinal, who would then sing out, '*Duos habet et bene pendentes*' ('He has two, and they dangle very well').

All such scurrilous stories would have been enjoyed in the eighteenth century, a time when anti-Papist feelings ran strong. The card game was played for money and involved up to eight players. Apart from a special staking board with separate compartments, it required a pack of cards from which the eight of diamonds had been removed. The dealer would start by 'dressing the board' – that is to say, by placing six counters in the compartment marked 'Pope' (representing the nine of diamonds), two counters in both 'matrimony' and 'intrigue' and one counter each in 'ace', 'king', 'queen', 'jack' and 'game'. The aim of the game was to win counters by playing cards that corresponded to the labelled compartments and to be the first to run out of cards. That person won the counters in 'game' and also one counter from each player for each card they held in their hand. At the end of an agreed number of rounds the counters were translated into money. The game remained popular well into the Victorian era, and the staking boards can occasionally be found in junk shops, usually made of papier mâché or tin.

70. The Prince of Wales Caused a Tartan Mania

In the 150 years after the Restoration, not one reigning monarch deigned to set foot north of the border into Scotland, notwithstanding the fact that the kingdoms were united. Such reticence may have been with good reason – the rebellions of 1715 and 1745, followed up by brutal persecution, the Highland Clearances and the decline of the clan system, had left many Scots bitterly opposed to the Union. But over time, such feelings were replaced by a yearning for a version of Scottishness that had never really existed – the romanticised Scotland of Walter Scott and his novel *Waverley*.

It was against this background that, within a year of his coronation, George IV decided to head north at the suggestion of the newly ennobled Sir Walter. It was an excuse for the reinvention of a Scottish identity, complete with the ubiquitous tartan kilt. Anyone who witnessed the elevation of a fairly obscure item of exclusively Highland dress into a national costume would have been astonished. With typical gusto, His Majesty set about ordering a complete costume from outfitters in Edinburgh, at a staggering cost of over £1,300. Naturally, for that cost he didn't just get a bright-red, royal tartan: he got the works, with dirk, sword, pistols and 'bling' – gold chains and buckles galore. The problem was that the king didn't really have the legs for a kilt, especially as he chose to wear it immodestly short, therefore he added his own personal touch to the ensemble: a pair of pink tights.

Sir Walter Scott had already lined up the leading Scottish families, from both the Highlands and the Lowlands, to prepare them for the new spirit of nationalism which would accompany the king's visit. No matter that the Dress Act of 1746 had forbidden the wearing of traditional highland garb, or that the kilt had never been more than a form of thick plaid worn by outlaws in the more mountainous regions of the country. No matter that the kilt was never the traditional Scottish garb so favoured by modern-day filmmakers. (This was just as inaccurate as the anachronism of warriors wearing blue woad on their faces – a habit which had died out nearly two millennia earlier).The idea of a 'clan tartan' was invented, thereby giving a huge boost to the Scottish textile industry. Prior to that date, most cloth was woven by hand, using wools coloured according to the availability of natural dyes, such as those obtained from berries, bracken, tree bark and certain plants. Those colours changed according to the seasons, and therefore there was never a tradition of specific colours for specific clans – they wore whatever the weaver came up with. The visit of the king in August 1822 was a huge success, with balls, levées and banquets marking what was termed at the time as 'one and twenty daft days'. Enthusiastic crowds mobbed the king wherever he went. Scottishness was reborn, and has thrived ever since.

71. Bridges Didn't Last Forever

For over six centuries there was a bridge over the River Thames. London Bridge was not just *a* bridge, it was *the* bridge: the only crossing. Perhaps 100,000 people a day were using it during the early part of the eighteenth century, and not just pedestrians. Add in the coaches and the waggons, as well as the innumerable sheep and cattle being driven to market, and there would have been a non-stop flow of traffic in both directions.

The problem was that the bridge was a hopeless bottleneck, both on land and on the river. It was described as a wall with holes in it because there were so many pillars separated by narrow gaps, which led to strong currents. Ships could only pass for a few hours either side of high tide, meaning that those waiting to be unloaded were stuck in the Pool of London for days on end, waiting for their turn to pass through. This in turn provided opportunities for theft and smuggling.

For pedestrians and horse riders, the bridge was a hopeless constriction. The shops and homes which straddled the bridge in a higgledy-piggledy fashion caused endless delays and narrowed the carriageway. Tolls to restrict access were tried, without success, along with a 'keep to the right' system aimed at reducing congestion. After 1758, the Corporation of London demolished all the buildings on the bridge, doubling the width of the carriageway, and took down the medieval gates which were causing an obstruction. The central arch was removed and a new Great Arch constructed, enabling shipping to pass much more easily. The river was safer for everyone, but just as the commissioners were congratulating themselves on their foresight, more bills started to come in, especially after hard winters when frost and ice caused extensive damage to the structure of the bridge, particularly below the waterline.

The decision was made to replace the old bridge, despite opposition from many Londoners who were horrified at the destruction of an old landmark. A competition was held in 1799. One of the designs was submitted by Thomas Telford, but his scheme for a single-span, iron bridge was dismissed as being impracticable. The competition was won by John Rennie, with his design for a new, streamlined bridge constructed out of granite to be brought up to London from Haytor in Devon. It would be erected just 30 yards from the old bridge, and work was started in 1824. The following year saw the laying of the foundation stone by the new King George IV inside the southern coffer-dam. Work finished in 1831 and the new bridge was officially opened in the presence of King William IV and his wife, Queen Adelaide, on 1 August 1831. Following this, the old bridge was dismantled, stone by stone. The new Rennie Bridge was to last 150 years until it too was dismantled. It can now be seen as a tourist attraction at Lake Havasu, in the middle of the Arizona desert.

72. There Were Various Attempts to Assassinate George III

'Good King George' survived several attempts on his life, including one which occurred on 2 August 1786 as he was alighting from his carriage. A woman called Margaret Nicholson lunged at him with an ivory-handled fruit knife, after appearing to try and hand him a petition. In fact, it was a blank piece of paper. She was disarmed and carted off to be tried for treason, but was found to be insane. She had originally come to London as a maid in various well-to-do establishments, but in 1782 she had been dismissed from her employment after a love affair with a fellow servant, and she had fallen on hard times. Her lover abandoned her, and she was left with a burning sense of injustice, becoming mentally unstable. She was sent to Bethlehem Royal Hospital (Bedlam) where she spent the rest of her miserable life. Her treatment would have been harsh, as in the 1800s inmates were shackled hand, neck and foot. It was fashionable for gentry to come and gawp at the poor unfortunates as they languished in Bedlam – part of the tourist scene of London.

Another two assassination attempts both occurred on 15 May 1800. In the first, a shot was fired at the king as he reviewed the troops in Hyde Park. The shot missed him, and hit and injured a naval clerk standing nearby. Unperturbed, the king accompanied his wife to the theatre that evening. He arrived at the theatre to a packed audience, who all stood for the playing of 'God Save the King'. In the audience was a deranged former soldier called Hadfield, who believed that, by dying, he would herald Christ's Second Coming. His cunning plan to bring about his own death was to shoot the king and be sent to the gallows for treason.

The story goes that he had suffered a number of severe sabre wounds to the head while serving in the British Army. Whatever the cause, he was clearly a total nutter and not a very good shot. One of the slugs missed its target by 14 inches, the other brought down flakes of plaster from the ceiling of the royal box. Hadfield was seized and dragged away, and the play continued, because, to the great admiration of all present, the king insisted that 'the show must go on'. He apparently enjoyed the play so much he fell asleep in the second half.

Hadfield's trial for treason was halted by the judge, who said that the medical evidence meant that the verdict would inevitably mean an acquittal, because it was quite obvious that the man was completely mad. The difficulty was that the criminally insane were usually handed back to their families to be looked after; Hadfield could hardly be let loose to wander the streets. Parliament quickly passed the Criminal Lunatics Act. This enabled prisoners who were found to be criminally insane to be locked up indefinitely, and Hadfield was carted off to Bedlam.

73. JAMES COX HAD A MUSEUM THAT EVERYONE WANTED TO SEE

James Cox was so much more than a jeweller, a clockmaker and a showman: he was a man with a vision. Although he failed in his mission to develop trade with the Far East and to establish Great Britain as the jewellery-making capital of the world, at least he tried.

For many years, he had been selling clocks and musical automata at the Sign of the Golden Urn, near Fleet Street. Small, intricately worked novelties were produced for sale in the Far East, where they were known as 'sing-songs'. Cox also supplied rather more elaborate pieces to the royal households of Europe, and from there to the imperial palaces in Russia and China and to the Great Mogul in India. It got to the stage that only an emperor could afford his incredibly intricate pieces. As the German writer and traveller Auschenholz wrote at the time,

> Nothing which was not adorned with gold, silver and precious stones, had any attraction for them ... his project therefore was to join the magic of art to the imposing appearance of riches.

At one stage, Cox boasted that he was employing no fewer than 1,000 jewellers in London alone – an exaggeration perhaps, but it gives some idea of the scale of his enterprise. Auschenholz continues,

> Cox was resolved to send this collection to Asia: he however kept it nine years in London, and shewed the whole by means of tickets at 1/2 guinea each ... Never

was taste and grandeur, all the skills of mechanicks, and the magic of optics, united in such a high degree of perfection.

Entering his premises, known as the Spring Gardens Museum, in the 1770s, visitors were met with a golden dais surmounted by full-length portraits of the king and queen, painted by Zoffany. Salons led through to displays of birds and wild animals, all made of precious metals and studded with gemstones. The birds sang melodiously and flapped their wings, sending sparkles of light off their plumage encrusted with diamonds and rubies. A life-sized tiger covered in rare jewels turned its head to gaze at the visitors.

The most popular exhibit was the silver swan, with a mechanism made by Merlin, mentioned later. Its cleverly articulated neck and moving parts enthralled audiences, who seemed perfectly willing to pay the modern equivalent of £40 for admission and the same again for a catalogue.

Cox overstretched himself: his project to sell solid-silver castles 6 feet high, each 'a palace in fairy land', failed to elicit orders. No one could afford to buy his stock, and Parliament was asked to approve a scheme enabling Cox to operate a private lottery. Not enough tickets were sold, and most of the items had to be auctioned off or melted down. Bankruptcy swiftly followed, but Cox's works can still be seen in the Royal Collection. The Hermitage has one of his most spectacular creations, a 10-foot-high Peacock Clock, which was brought to Saint Petersburg in 1781.

74. One Man Doubled the Size of the Solar System

Sir Frederick William Herschel was one of the giants of the Georgian age. He did what no one had done for thousands of years before him – he discovered a planet, and in so doing set the whole science of astronomy on its head. The discovery doubled the size of the known solar system. He also discovered two of Saturn's moons and was the first to notice infra-red radiation. Not content with that, he designed and made the world's biggest telescope in his back garden. Oh, and he catalogued around 2,400 new stars (which he called nebulae) and, if that didn't fill his nights sufficiently, he also composed a couple of dozen symphonies, a number of oboe concertos and a harpsichord sonata.

He had originally come to Britain as a nineteen-year-old and took a job in Bath teaching music. In 1780 he was made director of the Bath orchestra. Music had taken second place to his hobby, astronomy, and he was apparently spending up to sixteen hours a day polishing his reflective mirrors and looking at the stars. In this work he was aided by his sister, the diminutive Caroline Herschel. In March 1781, he identified the new planet, and originally called it Georgium Sidum (literally 'George's Star', which was a bit fanciful given that he knew what he had found was a planet and not a star). The international scientific community (particularly the French) were never going to allow it be called that, and decided on the name Uranus. However, George III was so delighted with the compliment that he made Herschel his personal astronomer and awarded him a pension of £200 for life, which enabled him to give up teaching and concentrate all his efforts on observing the universe. He was awarded the Copley Medal, made a member the Royal Society and, finally, was knighted in 1816. He was also given a swathe of other awards by the international scientific community.

In 1785 he moved to Slough with his sister and was busy selling his polished mirrors to other astronomers throughout Europe and building his own telescopes (he made some 400 during his lifetime). The largest of all these telescopes was a 40-foot monster which he constructed in his garden. There were, of course, no planning controls in those days! He specialised in observing and cataloguing double or binary stars, observing their relative positions over a quarter of a century and establishing that they moved under mutual gravitational attraction.

Herschel was the first person to work out that the solar system was moving through space and that the Milky Way was disc-shaped. He coined the word asteroid to describe moons and minor planets. He also observed sunspots on the surface of the sun, speculating that this was evidence of a solar life form. He helped found the Royal Astronomical Society in 1820 and lived long enough to hand over the baton of astronomical discoveries to his son, John.

75. EVERYONE LOOKED TO THE SKIES IN 1784 – AND MANY HAD THEIR POCKETS PICKED

When the Montgolfier brothers took to the skies in November 1783 in a hot-air balloon, they were followed a mere fortnight later by a fellow Frenchman called Jacques Alexander Cesar Charles in a balloon filled with hydrogen. To Charles should go the credit for the idea of the wicker basket, the netting to keep the balloon stable and the valve-and-ballast system to help control altitude. When his balloon, called the *Charlière*, took to the skies at the Tuileries Gardens in Paris, it did so in front of a vast concourse of people – it is reported that half the population of Paris, some 400,000 people, saw the successful launch.

News of this astounding event quickly crossed the Channel and within weeks everyone wanted to be a part of the craze. Balloon mania swept the country. One of the earliest to experiment in England was the remarkable Dr Jenner (he of vaccination fame). In September 1784, he launched a hydrogen-filled balloon from the grounds of Berkeley Castle. The *Gloucester Journal* of 6 September 1784 noted,

> On Thursday last at two o'clock a balloon was launched from the inner court of Berkeley Castle, which rose to a very great height, and was visible for a quarter of an hour. The same afternoon it was seen to descend in a field where some people were reaping, near the Smith's shop, in the parish of Kingscote, about ten miles from Berkeley. The reapers were so much terrified, that they could not for some time be prevailed upon to approach it.

Ballooning soon became a craze that got out of hand

– the *Public Advertiser* of 13 September 1784 issuing the warning,

> The Balloon Mania, it is feared, will not subside, till some fatal calamity shall be the result of it. One of these balloons, filled with turpentine and other matter of that kind, falling last night on the leads of a house in Tottenham Court Road, the leads melted by the fire … Within these few days more than fifty have been sent off from Westminster and its vicinity.

One of the early pioneers in this country was the Italian aeronaut Vincent Lunardi. Among the crowd of 200,000 gathered to see him take to the skies from the Artillery Ground in September 1784 was the Prince of Wales. Lunardi became something of an early celebrity, and stories of his exploits filled the newspapers and inspired countless caricatures. Images of balloons were used to decorate everything from snuff boxes to clocks and furniture. Children experimented with making their own balloons using lighted candles inside paper bags, and such toys posed a very real fire risk to owners of thatched houses. Balloon mania really only lasted a couple of years, but crowds would always turn out to watch an ascent, and pickpockets quickly learned that while everyone was looking to the skies, concentrating on the balloon, it was an ideal time to pick a pocket or two.

76. Everyone Had Their Favourite Hobby in 1819

If you had been wandering around London in 1818 and 1819 it would have been impossible not to have observed a new hobby sweeping the capital – even if the observation was made as you hurled yourself to the ground in an effort to get out of the way. The hobby? Well, that was it: the hobby, hobby horse, dandy horse or pedestrian curricle.

It was invented in 1817 by a German living in France by the name of Baron Karl von Drais. For that reason the early velocipede, the forerunner of the bicycle, was called a draisine, or *draisienne* in France. The problem was that it was made of wood and iron and weighed 48 pounds! Nevertheless, gentlemen saw it as a stylish way of travelling; it was quicker than walking, but, more importantly, it made an impression on the people you left trailing in your wake.

The fashion for propelling yourself around town on a hobby was introduced to Britain by the London coach-builder Denis Johnson. He made it a little lighter and used a serpentine frame. Even though the hobby horse had no pedals, no gears and no chain, you can clearly see the influences on the bicycle, which came into popularity later in the century. To move forward, the rider pushed on the ground with his feet, leaning forward while sitting on a central saddle. Without putting too fine a point on it, it must have been an extremely uncomfortable conveyance for gentlemen, especially if they were travelling over cobbled streets! But no matter, it was fashionable (hence 'dandy-horse'). They would have retailed for around £10 – quite a tidy sum for a bit of a gimmick. The other difficulty for purchasers was that the adjustable saddle had yet to be invented, which meant that the frame of the velocipede had to be more-or-less made to measure. That way, the rider could touch the ground effortlessly, whereas a frame which was too large or too small would have been hard to operate. Its inability to cope with rough road surfaces made many users switch to the smoother surfaces of the pavement. This outraged pedestrians and resulted in many areas passing Bye Laws restricting users of the contraption to the roads.

The hobby provoked a plethora of caricatures ridiculing the absurdity of the exponents of the art, and suggested that the age of the horse would soon be over, throwing vets, ostlers and farriers onto the scrap heap. However, the hobby disappeared almost as quickly as it arrived. Within a couple of years they were a thing of the past. So what happened? This may have been because the fashion for riding hobbies could not translate to uneven country roads, and, no doubt, because wearing fashionably tight trousers made for an extremely painful riding position! No one wanted to be seen on 'last year's fad' and the craze disappeared into obscurity.

77. Dr Johnson Had the Last Word in Lexicography

Dr Samuel Johnson had published his original *Dictionary of the English Language* in April 1755. For 150 years his dictionary was the pre-eminent source of words, their meaning, pronunciation and use. Many of the editions that followed shamelessly used the name 'Dr Johnson' as part of their title and then simply listed the words which he had selected in his original, two-volume set. They often missed off the full meanings of words and omitted examples of quotations that were the hallmark of the original work.

Poor Johnson – he had originally been a teacher in Lichfield in Staffordshire, but apparently his pupils did not appreciate his teaching skills. Indeed, it is quite possible that he suffered from Tourette's Syndrome, with complaints about his 'oddities of manner and uncouth gesticulation'. Throughout his life he suffered from a tic, emphasised by him uttering strange noises 'as if clucking like a hen' or exhaling air 'like a whale'. These oddities of manner forced him to move to London in 1737 and for the next decade he scraped a fairly miserable living as a Grub Street hack, struggling to keep his creditors at bay. Fortunately, he had been befriended by the actor David Garrick (indeed the latter had probably been a pupil of his), and Garrick effected numerous introductions for him. Eventually, he was asked by the bookseller Robert Dodsley to compile a definitive dictionary of the English language. It was not the first attempt – there had been a score of earlier versions spread over the preceding 200 years, but Johnson took things to an entirely new level of erudition and scholarship. The Earl of Chesterfield agreed to act as patron of the project and to pay Johnson the huge fee of 1,500 guineas.

Booksellers wanted a definitive work that would lay down rules of spelling and usage. In their view, the language was in a mess. Johnson agreed that language needed to be controlled, and actually thought that it could be stopped from evolving by laying down strict rules. To that extent his masterpiece failed miserably. In other ways, his methodology and intellectual approach inspired and influenced subsequent lexicographers.

Whereas the French had their forty 'immortals' (a committee of learned men who made up the Académie Française, and who would take upwards of fifty-five years to compile their *Dictionnaire*), Johnson set to with just half a dozen clerical assistants, and completed the whole task in a little over eight years. The work was not just a collection of over 42,000 words: it gave definitions and included examples of how and when those words were used in English literature, with tens of thousands of quotations.

Johnson ended his days gout-ridden and in great pain. He was buried in Westminster Abbey on Christmas Eve 1784. A myriad of pocket editions intended for school use appeared shortly after Johnson's death. They sold in their thousands, both in England and overseas, with editions being printed throughout the nineteenth century.

78. Matthew Boulton Made a Mint – the Royal Mint

Matthew Boulton was a powerhouse of the Industrial Revolution. What was all the more remarkable was that he never had any formal scientific training. From running the family metalworking business in Birmingham, he progressed to consolidating his engineering works at the Soho Manufactory, opened in 1765, and there he produced huge quantities of metal goods, including items made of ormolu (gilt bronze) and silver plate. A great range of commodities were made in his factory, from snuff boxes to candlesticks, cameo brooches to buckles and tinder boxes to enamelware. These items used to be called 'toys' – a term which included such things as nutmeg graters, toothpick cases and small metal knick-knacks. Boutlon was aware of the problems faced by silversmiths in having to send all their finished products off to London to be assayed. This was especially sensitive if the products were made to a new design and where there was a risk of items being copied or damaged. To overcome the difficulty, in 1773 Boulton successfully petitioned Parliament to create the Birmingham Assay, giving a huge boost to Midlands silversmiths by enabling them to operate independently of their London counterparts.

Boulton married a distant cousin, but when his wife died he controversially married her sister – a highly unusual union not permitted under Ecclesiastical Law, but perfectly legal under Common Law. They went on to have three children.

In 1775, he entered into a partnership with James Watt, supplying hundreds of steam-powered engines to mines and factories across the entire country. Boulton opened his Soho Mint in 1788, using eight steam-driven machines of his own design. For a while he made many of the copper tokens commissioned by tradesmen seeking to get round the shortage of low denomination coins in general circulation. The problem was that the Royal Mint had not produced copper coinage for over forty years, and the coins in circulation were worn, underweight and subject to counterfeiting. Boulton was eventually granted a contract to produce coins for the Royal Mint, manufacturing the distinctive (and huge) 'cartwheel' pennies and two-pennies, all dated 1797. These heavyweights contained 1 and 2 ounces of copper respectively, and if that didn't leave a hole in your pocket you were highly fortunate!

45 million cartwheel coins were produced, and the powerful Boulton and Watt engines were introduced when the Royal Mint moved in 1805 from its historic site inside the Tower of London to new premises a few hundred yards away.

Above all, Boulton harnessed power – the power of steam, remarking to the diarist James Boswell on one of his visits to the Soho Works, 'I sell here, sir, what all the world desires to have – power.' He was a major philanthropist in the Midlands, helping to found and run the Birmingham General Hospital, a theatre, a choral society and a general dispensary. He died in 1809 and is commemorated, with James Watt, on the present £50 note.

79. Buckingham Palace Was the Queen's House

In 1703, the Duke of Buckingham built himself a town house on the site of mulberry gardens laid out by James I. His descendant, Sir Charles Sheffield, sold it to George III in 1761 for the sum of £21,000. Newly married, the king wanted it as a private residence for his wife, and it was accordingly called the Queen's House. Fourteen of Queen Charlotte's fifteen children were born there. George III still regarded St James's Palace as his official and ceremonial residence, and although the Queen's House was hardly palatial, it fitted the bill as a nursery for the royal brood. It was only in the Victorian age that the east wing was added, thereby creating an inner courtyard and the famous balcony from which the reigning monarch acknowledges the crowds massed in The Mall. In the eighteenth century it was a rambling home with poor ventilation, hopelessly inadequate heating and lighting and a singular lack of sanitary fittings.

On his accession, George IV adopted plans to make it into a palace fit for a king. The upgrade cost a fortune, using the neoclassical designs of John Nash. Parliament approved a budget of £150,000, but the costs were treble this. Indeed, John Nash was sacked once the cost exceeded £500,000, and the king never moved in. Even William IV never lived in the bottomless pit that was Buckingham Palace, and it was not until Queen Victoria came to the throne in 1837 that it actually became the official residence of the reigning monarch.

80. Mary Wollstonecraft Was the Mother of Frankenstein

Mary Wollstonecraft was an important feminist writer, but her reputation was ruined shortly after she died when her husband published the *Memoirs of the Author of A Vindication of the Rights of Woman*. The memoirs gave details of Mary's earlier affairs, her illegitimate child and much else. They appeared in 1798 and the public were appalled.

She had certainly led an unconventional life. Her father had a violent temper and was financially incompetent. When she left home she became a lady's companion, and then a governess, before making the extraordinarily brave decision to try and make a living as an author, initially writing book reviews. She fell head-over-heels in love with the married artist Henry Fuseli, but he rejected her suggestion that he and his wife should invite her to join their household to create a platonic threesome. Deeply depressed, she went to Paris in 1790 and published a pamphlet entitled *A Vindication of the Rights of Men* in response to Edmond Burke's *Reflections on the Revolution in France*. It was a passionate and intellectual attack on hereditary privilege and advocated republicanism. It was an instant success and was followed up by her even more important work, the seminal *A Vindication of the Rights of Women*.

While in revolutionary France she started a passionate affair with an American adventurer called Gilbert Imlay, becoming pregnant by him. She wanted to settle down to a life of domesticated bliss with her paramour, but it was not to be. Imlay found the domesticity stifling and walked out on her. Life for an unmarried mother in revolutionary France must have been very difficult, especially after 1793 when war between France and Britain broke out. She was in danger of being imprisoned or even guillotined, and in 1795 she returned to London with her baby to try and persuade Imlay to resume their affair. He refused and she attempted suicide. Hoping to ingratiate herself with Imlay by recovering money due to him from a business venture, she embarked on a trip to Scandinavia, taking her baby with her. She went on to publish the story of her travels as *Letters Written During a Short Residence in Sweden, Norway, and Denmark*.

Eventually, she fell in love again, this time with the English anarchist William Godwin. She became pregnant, and they married in 1797, living in adjoining houses in order to preserve their independence. Tragically, Mary died of puerperal fever at the age of thirty-eight, ten days after giving birth to a daughter, who was called Mary Wollstonecraft Godwin. The baby grew up to become a seventeen-year-old, headstrong rebel who eloped with the married poet Percy Bysshe Shelley. She went on to become a novelist, travel writer and essayist, with her most famous novel, *Frankenstein*, being published in 1818. She married Shelley after the suicide of his first wife.

Her mother would have been proud of her daughter's erratic and controversial lifestyle, which in so many ways mirrored her own.

81. Hannah More Showed That Women Counted – and Could Read Too, If Schooled

Hannah More was a social reformer, educationalist and an effective abolitionist. She was also a playwright, poet and pamphleteer, as well as being a philanthropist. Her life demonstrated that women could have a voice in the male-dominated eighteenth century. Hannah was the fourth of Jacob More's five daughters, and was born in 1745 in Bristol. Jacob had hoped to make it as a Church of England vicar, but ended up as an excise officer, before teaching at a small school. Hannah received an unusually rigorous education, mostly from her father and elder sisters, learning mathematics, Latin and French, instead of the more usual female accomplishments of piano playing, needlework and housekeeping. When Jacob opened a boarding school for girls in 1758 she attended the school as a pupil and later stayed on to become a teacher.

She enjoyed some success as a playwright but suffered a nervous breakdown when her engagement to a Somerset man called William Turner was broken off (after eight years and not a wedding band in sight). He agreed to pay her an annuity of £200, giving her sufficient financial independence to concentrate on her literary career. She proved to be rather popular as a writer, and her output included plays, poems and prose. She wrote many ethical and philosophical tracts, culminating in her *Cheap Repository Tracts*, which were published as a series: three per month during the fifteen-year period from 1795. Over 2 million of these pamphlets were sold, with their theme of frugality, sobriety and hard work. She lived to the age of eighty-eight and during her life was a friend of many of the most influential literary, philosophical and artistic figures of the time, from David Garrick and Samuel Johnson, to William Wilberforce, Edmund Burke and Joshua Reynolds. She was a regular member of the Blue Stockings Society, which met to discuss literary and intellectual matters and was unusually dominated by women.

In 1787 she met the evangelical clergyman John Newton (abolitionist and author of the hymn 'Amazing Grace'), along with other members of the Clapham sect. She started to use her public voice to help spread awareness of the horrors of slavery, particularly with her 1788 offering 'Slavery, a Poem'.

Two years before this she had bought a house at Cowslip Green in Wrington, near Bristol, with her sister Martha. Together they formed a dozen schools throughout the Mendips, aimed at teaching the illiterate poor from farming families. The proposal was not without opposition, not least from the farmers, but she was encouraged by Wilberforce to persevere. The girls were taught to read but not to write. Studying the Bible and the catechism was the sole purpose of their schooling, but at least it was a start. Hannah died in September 1833. She lived long enough to gain the satisfaction of seeing the Abolition of Slavery Act come into force just before her death.

82. ADMISSION TO ALMACK'S WAS THE TRUE MARK OF SOCIAL STATUS

To modern eyes, the success of Almack's is something of a mystery. Why should a club which was notorious for serving stale bread and butter, dry biscuits and no alcohol succeed in an age of excessive food and drink consumption? How on earth did it attain a pinnacle whereby admission to Almack's had more caché than receiving an invitation to the palace?

It started life as Almack's Assembly Rooms in 1764, when a Scot by the name of MacCall decided to open premises in King Street, St James's. He was reportedly nervous that his Scottish name might deter the punters, so he (in effect) reversed the syllables and called the place Almack's. The exterior of the Assembly Rooms was relatively understated, consisting of a Palladian-style building on three floors. Inside there were supper rooms, where guests were served either tea or lemonade and offered thinly sliced, day-old bread, or what was called 'dry' cake – that is to say, without icing. There was also a grand ballroom, resplendent with gold decorated pillars, large mirrors and impressive crystal chandeliers. By the end of the Regency period, candlelight had been replaced with gas lighting, and richly decorated panels with designs in the style of Robert Adam adorned the walls between the draperies. At one end of the ballroom was a raised dais, and it was here that those most despotic of creatures sat – the lady patronesses. These ladies were the arbiters of social standing and acceptability, and they gave the place its name for being the most sought-after marriage market in the land. These were the ruthless ladies who could make or break a family's aspirations. They could sniff out 'trade' at a hundred paces, and 'trade' was most definitely not admitted.

Money alone was not enough to earn a ticket to one of the balls – you had to have breeding, class and education. You had to dress elegantly (in the early days Beau Brummel helped establish the dress code), and you also had to be able to dance and exhibit the appropriate social graces. You had to pass the scrutiny of the lady patronesses, who included at different times such luminaries as Lady Jersey, Lady Castlereagh, Lady Sefton and the waspish Countess Lieven. A more snobbish collection of bores is hard to imagine. Their favour was not easily bestowed and it could be removed capriciously, so that you might be 'in' one year and 'out' the next. The actual balls were held every Wednesday night in the season, which only lasted for twelve weeks, from early March to the start of June. Membership of Almack's cost 10 guineas, but members had to apply for a voucher for each separate ball they wished to attend at a cost of 10s a voucher. Almack's continued as an important social venue until 1871, when it was renamed Willis's Rooms, but it never regained the prestige it enjoyed in the Regency period.

83. THE LORD MAYOR'S CARRIAGE HAS NOT NEEDED AN MOT OR A ROAD LICENCE IN 250 YEARS

One of the highlights of the year was the Lord Mayor's Show. It was a street celebration, a parade, a carnival and a procession to mark the inauguration of a new Lord Mayor of London, all rolled into one. At its heart, it was a simple procession from the Guildhall, via the Mansion House and St Paul's Cathedral, to the Royal Courts of Justice, where the new lord mayor swore allegiance to the king.

For centuries it had been a noisy, vibrant pageant, not least because all the apprentices were given the day off (cue much drunken behaviour and high jinks). The lord mayor was (and is) chosen by members of the livery companies meeting at London's Guildhall on the nearest weekday to Michaelmas Day (29 September). Candidates were city aldermen, all of whom must have served as sheriff. The day after the new lord mayor had been sworn in, the procession took place. It was always attended by the Great Twelve Livery Companies (the Goldsmiths, Haberdashers, Mercers, Fishmongers, Grocers and so on). The other livery companies took part by invitation, and each took it in turns to arrange the pageant when it was their representative who was elected lord mayor. The pageant was originally held annually on 29 October, but the adoption of the Gregorian calendar in 1751 moved the date by eleven days. For the next two centuries it was held on 9 November.

Traditionally, the lord mayor made the journey on horseback, but there was an unfortunate incident in 1710 when the lord mayor was unseated by an overenthusiastic and somewhat drunken flower girl; the lord mayor broke his leg. Ensuing years saw the journey being made by river, with a flotilla of decorated barges (hence 'floats') accompanying the official barge on its trip along the Thames. It was a scene painted on various occasions by Canaletto and other artists, intent on recording what was already a major tourist attraction.

It wasn't until 1757 that it was decided that the journey was safe to be made on land, as long as there was a suitable carriage to give protection from the drunken revellers. Enter Sir Charles Asgill, the wealthy banker who was to be lord mayor that year. He commissioned a new state coach to be built at a cost of just over £1,000, with elaborate gilded side panels decorated by Giovanni Cipriani. The coach itself was built by Joseph Berry of Holborn, and the cost was covered by a contribution of £60 from each of the livery companies. The lord mayor himself chipped in, with a personal contribution of £100. The coach is still in use today, more than two and a half centuries after it was first commissioned, and it is generally credited as being the oldest ceremonial vehicle in the world still in regular use. One anachronism: brakes were added in 1951.

84. Merlin Invented the Roller Skate, but Not the Brake for It

I give you Mr John Joseph Merlin, a splendid fellow born near Maastricht, in Belgium, in 1735. He certainly knew how to make a grand entrance; on one occasion he entered a ballroom on roller skates (of his own invention) while playing the fiddle. As a contemporary report mentions, 'When not having provided the means of retarding his velocity, or commanding its direction, he impelled himself against a mirror of more than £500 value, dashed it to atoms, broke his instrument to pieces and wounded himself most severely.' There was, however, rather more to Mr Merlin than inventing skates-without-brakes. He was an inventor, a showman, a fine musician, a clockmaker and much more besides. He studied for six years as a maker of clocks, automata and mathematical and musical instruments in Paris, before coming to England in 1760. He never went home. He set to and developed many refinements to existing musical instruments: the harp, the harpsichord, the new-fangled pianoforte, the barrel organ and so on.

By 1766 he had become James Cox's 'chief mechanic', developing the mechanism for the famous silver swan, mentioned earlier. You can still see the brilliant action as the swan appears to turn its head from side to side before lowering it into the water and swallowing a fish! Obviously no one told Merlin that swans are vegetarian.

Merlin decided to set up on his own. He acquired premises near Oxford Street in 1783, and he called the place Merlin's Mechanical Museum. What visitors saw was an impressive array of automata and various inventions made by Merlin. One of the people attending the exhibition was a young schoolboy from Devon called Charles Babbage. The story goes that Merlin took the boy upstairs to see his workshop and to show some more exotic automata. Clearly the sight had a profound influence on Babbage. Years later he recalled that one of the automata was 'an admirable danseuse, with a bird on the forefinger of her right hand, which wagged its tail, flapped its wings and opened its beak'. Babbage was completely gobsmacked. Fired up by this visit, he would later go on and invent the forerunner of the modern computer.

Merlin was a prolific inventor of a wide array of indispensable items. He came up with various inventions to help the disabled – a self-propelled gouty chair, a mechanical prosthetic hand and a set of whist cards for the blind. He invented an odometer called a 'way-wise' and a bell communication system to summon servants. There was a clock running on atmospheric pressure (and which therefore was an attempt at perpetual motion), followed by an automated gambling wheel, a mechanical garden and a fairground carousel.

Merlin died at Paddington in 1803 at the age of sixty-eight. In his will he directed that his thirty-year-old horse should be shot. Having died unmarried, he left his property to two brothers and a sister.

85. Thomas Clarkson Was the True Father of Abolition

Think abolition and we tend to think of William Wilberforce, which is a bit hard on the single-minded Thomas Clarkson. He was the real powerhouse behind abolition. If Wilberforce was the mouthpiece of the movement, Clarkson was the engine, devoting years of his life to travelling tens of thousands of miles around the country obtaining evidence, canvassing, educating and basically giving Wilberforce the bullets to fire in Parliament.

Throughout the last half of the eighteenth century there had been a growing groundswell of opinion against slavery. Parliament did not lead the change, but reacted to the continual pressure from people like Thomas Clarkson. Along with two other Anglicans, Clarkson was a founder member of the Society for Effecting the Abolition of the Slave Trade. The other nine founder members were Quakers, but Quakers were banned from entering Parliament, and they therefore sought the support of William Wilberforce, MP for Kingston upon Hull. Clarkson's involvement started when he was at Cambridge University. The twenty-five-year-old had entered an essay-writing competition (in Latin) on the question, 'Is it lawful to enslave the unconsenting?' The research for the essay was to change his life. It dawned on him that someone had to do something about the appalling, degrading trade and that the someone was going to be him.

The essay was translated into English and it became widely circulated and acclaimed. He tirelessly toured the country on horseback, organising petitions and rallies and collecting evidence in the form of first-hand accounts from sailors in ports such as Liverpool and Bristol. He pestered and cajoled William Wilberforce into promoting the abolitionist cause in Parliament. Clarkson collected and distributed stories of the hideous squalor on board the slave ships, showing people his gruesome collection of torture implements. It proved to be a most effective use of visual aids, a marketing tool which we nowadays take for granted.

Wilberforce first tried to push his anti-slavery bill through Parliament in 1791, but was crushingly defeated. Soon, all attention was devoted to the war with France. The anti-slavery movement was obliged to hibernate until war was nearly over, before redoubling its efforts. In 1804, Clarkson again hit the road, criss-crossing the countryside, whipping up support. Finally, the Slave Trade Act became law in 1807, making it illegal to engage in the slave trade throughout the British colonies. In the following year, Clarkson published his *History of the Abolition of the African Slave Trade*. He then devoted his time to supporting moves to end slavery in all parts of the world, and was the main speaker at the inaugural meeting of the Anti-Slavery Society (now called Anti-Slavery International) in 1840.

Wilberforce continues to be remembered and gets all the credit – his is a household name. Clarkson is a forgotten hero, dying in 1846. Wilberforce is buried in Westminster Abbey near his political chum, William Pitt (the Younger); Clarkson is interred at St Mary's Church in the small Suffolk village of Playford.

86. All That Glittered Was Not Necessarily Gold, or Silver

One of the remarkable things about the eighteenth century was the way people came up with inventions that brought luxury items into everyday circulation. One such person was the Sheffield cutler Thomas Boulsover, who, in 1743, stumbled upon a process that became known as Sheffield plate. Suddenly, it was possible to make high-quality, decorative items that looked like silver, but at a fraction of the cost. Boulsover discovered that if you heated a 'sandwich' of metal made by putting a piece of copper between two thin sheets of silver, the two metals fused together when heat was applied. This could then be milled out to produce a single sheet of metal. At first, Boulsover confined his manufacturing to what he knew best – the making of buttons – but others saw the potential and were soon using the metal to make small boxes, jugs, candlesticks and coffee pots. The technique was put to good use by industrialists like Matthew Boulton, mentioned earlier, and remained popular until 1840 when electroplating took its place. Meanwhile, Thomas Boulsover continued to live in Sheffield until his death in 1788, aged eighty-three.

Another inventor of cheap substitute metal was Christopher Pinchbeck. If you look up 'pinchbeck' in a dictionary it gives you 'a cheap imitation, something spurious', which is a tad unfair on the man who gave his name to an alloy consisting of three parts zinc and four parts copper. Christopher Pinchbeck was a watchmaker and a jeweller, and he was looking for an alloy that looked like gold but was cheap and easy to produce and would therefore be suitable for making what we would now call costume jewellery. In doing so he made jewellery and pocket watches much more affordable. It meant that travellers wary of being held up at gunpoint could safely wear low-cost and replaceable jewellery. After all, why take your finest jewels with you on a journey when indistinguishable substitutes would serve your purpose?

Pinchbeck successfully made watch cases out of alloy, bringing down the cost of timepieces dramatically, and he sold them at places like Southwark Fair. There was no attempt at deception: he described them as being 'chased in so curious a manner as not to be distinguished by the nicest eye from real gold', but in time the word pinchbeck became a pejorative term because unscrupulous traders manufactured inferior quality products and passed them off as gold.

In fact, Pinchbeck was a clever maker of automata and musical curiosities. He had burst onto the scene in London when he was already in his forties. According to an article in the *London Courant* of 1716, he was charging the astronomic fee of 700 guineas for one of his fancy instruments. He moved to Clerkenwell and made watches and clocks, specialising in incredibly ornate and complicated astronomical instruments. His eldest son Christopher took over the business, and he became King's Clockmaker by appointment to George III.

87. A Small Fishing Village Called Brighthelmstone Became Fashionable Brighton

In the Middle Ages Brighton was a prosperous fishing village called Brighthelmstone, with a population of 4,000 souls. Being razed to the ground by the French in the reign of Henry VIII set it back a bit, as did the Great Storm in 1703. This left the houses wrecked and covered in shingle. More violent storms followed, and it looked as though Brighton would disappear altogether. Then it slowly recovered, as doctors extolled the virtues of swimming, walking along in the bracing sea air and, curiously, of drinking seawater.

Prosperity spread slowly, and with it came public buildings. The first of two assembly rooms, one for dancing and the other for gambling at cards, was built in 1767. A small theatre had opened, as well as a grammar school in 1789. The population doubled between 1750 and 1783, but the real boost to the town was royal patronage. George III started a trend of visiting the South Coast, with Weymouth his favourite destination. His brother, the Duke of Cumberland, rented a holiday house in Brighton and the Prince of Wales, who had rather more in common with his rakish uncle, the duke, than with his tedious father, became a regular visitor. His first visit was in September 1783, and the town never looked back. Over the next forty years it became the most fashionable of resorts, with over 600 new homes being built in the last quarter of the century. In 1784, the young Prince of Wales rented a farmhouse in the town, anxious to get away from the tedium of life at Court under the watchful eye of George III. Here in Brighton he could let rip, and that is just what he did, throwing lavish parties. Here he was able to entertain his mistress, Maria Fitzherbert, the twice-widowed woman with whom he went through a civil marriage ceremony in 1785. The marriage was invalid under the terms of the Royal Marriages Act, because he had neither the consent of the king nor the Privy Council. Such consent was never likely to be given, in view of her Catholic sympathies.

The couple spent much of their spare time in Brighton, and the in-crowd of the day followed suit. Suddenly, the high-class hookers from London had somewhere to go to for a change of scenery, and business was brisk for the builders of the fine Georgian terraces, which sprang up along the seafront. In 1787 the prince started work on building the extraordinary royal residence that became the Brighton Pavilion, with construction spread over thirty-five years. It started out modestly enough, in the neoclassical style. Successive waves of building, latterly under the auspices of John Nash, produced a striking building with influences from China, India and goodness knows where else. It was still a popular residence when William IV succeeded his brother to the throne, but fell out of favour with Queen Victoria, who hated the place.

88. It Was No Fun Being an Animal

The Georgians were remarkably cruel to animals, right up until the passing of the Cruelty to Animals Act in 1835. The Act outlawed a variety of 'entertainments', including bear-baiting (where dogs would be set against a bear chained around its neck or feet) and bull-baiting (as in Stamford, in Lincolnshire, where it was traditional to drive a bull through town, tormenting and torturing it for twenty-four hours before chasing it into the river). Many of the more cruel sports were linked to gambling, especially cockfighting, where fortunes could be made and lost in side bets, even though the prize money may only have been a few guineas. Many towns had cockpits, and they were invariably in use on race days in order to give gentlemen a pretext for gambling during the times when horses were not actually being raced. The birds were fitted with lethally sharp steel blades in order to inflict maximum damage on their opponents. Other gambling events included setting a dog loose in a pit containing 100 rats and timing how long it took for all the vermin to be killed – and, on at least one occasion, setting two dogs loose inside a lion's cage for the 'sport' of seeing how long they would survive.

The public was fascinated by displays of exotic animals, and one of the most famous displays was at Exeter Change, off the Strand. Here, primates were kept in appalling, cramped conditions. The star of the show was an enormous bull elephant called Chunee. Having appeared in various theatrical productions, Chunee spent many years at the Change, entertaining the crowds with his party trick of picking up a coin in his trunk and handing it to the owner. The keepers were accustomed to walking the 7-ton elephant down the Strand – partly to give him exercise and partly to help drum up business – but one day in 1826 the elephant went berserk (it was probably in musth) and the decision was made to have the beast put down. Poison was tried. It failed. Over 150 musket balls were fired at him from point-blank range, but the *coup de grace* was administered with a harpoon. Afterwards, Chunee's hide was cut up and sold for souvenirs. The public were outraged, sparking letters to *The Times*. By then a group of individuals, which included William Wilberforce, had held a meeting in Old Slaughter's Coffee House, St Martin's Lane, to raise public awareness of animal welfare. In time the group grew into the Society for the Prevention of Cruelty to Animals. A decade later, after the society had become involved in a high-profile case aimed at ending the bull-baiting in Stamford, it achieved royal status and became known as the RSPCA. Meanwhile, the backlash against animal cruelty had led directly to the passing of the Cruelty to Animals Act and also gave impetus to the creation of the first Zoological Society. London Zoo in Regent's Park finally opened to the public in 1847.

89. There Were Two Brunels, and One of Them Was Georgian

Everyone knows about Isambard Kingdom Brunel, the man responsible for the Clifton Suspension Bridge, the Great Western Railway and the SS *Great Britain*. He was a Victorian hero, but who recalls his father, an engineer from the Georgian era who deserves to be better remembered?

Marc Isambard Brunel (from now on referred to as 'MIB') father of Isambard junior, and his assistant and guide on many of his projects, was born in France in 1769. Before the revolution he was a cadet in the French navy, but when Paris erupted with violence he was forced to flee to Rouen. He was a royalist and narrowly escaped imprisonment and death. From there he went to America, where he was appointed chief engineer to the city of New York, designing and overseeing the construction of various public buildings. While working on one of his projects, he heard of the problems faced by the British Navy in the manufacture of pulley blocks. This was a task for skilled men, each block being handmade by craftsmen. No fewer than a 100,000 such blocks were needed by the Navy each and every year. MIB devised a way of bringing mass-production techniques to the task, so that unskilled operators could churn out the blocks on machines specially designed for the purpose. He came to England, putting his own money into the project to the tune of £2,000, and was greatly helped by teaming up with Henry Maudslay (see later) who helped make the block-making machinery. The Navy seemed to prefer not to reward MIB for a number of years, but eventually paid him £17,000 in retrospective settlement of his claim. By then (1808), MIB was producing 130,000 blocks a year, thereby contributing directly to the defeat of the French fleet by the British Navy.

There followed various unprofitable ventures, causing him and his family to be thrown into the King's Bench Prison for debtors in Southwark, but eventually Parliament were persuaded to pay off his debts in return for MIB promising to drop his plans to emigrate to Russia. He stayed and started working on driving a tunnel under the Thames, using a special shield he had designed to enable thirty-six miners at any one time to work on the rock face deep under the riverbed. In places it was not quite deep enough, and there were problems with water pouring in to the tunnel as it was being worked. In 1843 it was finally completed; it was the first time that such a monumental project had been successfully carried out. That year, 1 million people visited the tunnel to inspect the 7.5 million bricks that lined the structure linking Rotherhithe and Wapping. In time, the tunnel was incorporated into the London Underground system.

MIB suffered a series of strokes and died aged eighty in 1849, having been knighted eight years earlier.

90. Edward Jenner, Smallpox Pioneer, Was an Authority on the Cuckoo

For a man credited with saving more lives than anyone else in history, and of leading to the first ever eradication of a disease that had previously plagued mankind, Edward Jenner was something of a polymath. He was interested in fossils, hot-air ballooning, heart disease and the cuckoo. Indeed, he had already been made a member of the Royal Society on the strength of the research he carried out on the nesting habits of the cuckoo, before he even started looking into immunisation, vaccines and cow pox. It was Jenner who established that the young cuckoo chick was responsible for ejecting its nest-mates, not the adult bird.

He was the son of an Anglican clergyman and received a good education, before being apprenticed as a fourteen-year-old to a surgeon in Chipping Sodbury. At the age of twenty-one he went away to study surgery and anatomy, before returning to his native village of Berkeley in Gloucestershire to become a country GP. He was personally familiar with the prevailing fashion of immunising against smallpox, because he had been immunised as a schoolboy. The method of immunisation, known as variolation, involved deliberately infecting a fit, healthy person with a supposedly mild strain of the disease by injecting the patient with matter taken from someone who had had a mild attack of smallpox. In Edward's case it meant a period of starvation and being shut up in a confined space with other boys, before being given a dose of the potentially fatal disease. The suffering of the patient varied hugely with variolation, and on some occasions the injected disease proved deadly.

As a GP, Jenner noticed that milkmaids often caught cowpox, but afterwards never caught smallpox, and he correctly surmised that the former gave an immunity against the latter. He began experimenting, and the story of Blossom the cow, Sarah Nelmes the milkmaid and James Phipps the gardener's son has gone down in history. Suffice to say that Master James had to patiently accept that his arms were being used as experimental pincushions. He was injected with a serum containing cow pox. Having been infected, he was then variolated against smallpox. Nothing happened. The experiment was repeated on a number of occasions, just to make sure that the immunity was permanent. It was also carried out on two dozen other human guinea pigs, before Jenner was ready to publish his findings. The result was a sensation and a source of controversy which lasted for decades. Not everyone accepted Jenner's ideas on vaccination – he was ridiculed and lampooned constantly, and it was years before his ideas on immunology were accepted. Defending his findings took up all his time, at the expense of his general practice, and in 1802 Parliament voted him a grant of £20,000, increased by another £10,000 once the Royal Society of Physicians accepted that his ideas on vaccination actually worked. He died aged seventy-three, in 1823.

91. NELSON WAS A LEGEND IN HIS OWN LIFETIME

Because Horatio Nelson became so famous in death at the Battle of Trafalgar, it is easy to forget that he was a national hero well before he set off on his final journey on board HMS *Victory* in 1803. He had been born in Norfolk in 1758, went to sea at twelve and became a captain at twenty. When war with France broke out in 1793 he joined the Mediterranean fleet, but was injured in a land-based skirmish at Calvi. A bullet struck a sandbag near Nelson's head, showering his face with grit and sand, causing him to lose the sight in his right eye. He distinguished himself in the Battle of Cape St Vincent in 1797, but was lucky to escape an official reprimand, having disobeyed direct orders. Later the same year he took part in a naval battle off Tenerife, when a musket ball shattered his right arm. The decision was made to amputate, but within an hour of the operation he had resumed command. The battle constituted a defeat for the British, but Nelson returned to a hero's welcome, not least because of his courage and personal injury. His victory in 1800 over the French fleet, in what became known as the Battle of the Nile, catapulted him to national fame. His brilliant tactics against a force with far greater firepower than his own destroyed the French navy and left Napoleon's army stranded in Egypt. His bravery, his seamanship, his nerves of steel and willingness to take huge risks endeared him to the public. Huge celebrations followed, and he was given the title of Baron of the Nile, showered with awards and voted a handsome pension by Parliament. His next posting was to Naples, where he met and fell in love with

Emma Hamilton, wife of the very-much-older William Hamilton. Neither of them wished to divorce their respective marriage partners, and Nelson took part in a curious *ménage à trois* when he moved in with the Hamiltons. The public were fascinated and scandalised in equal measure. Emma and Nelson went on to have a child together, called Horatia, born in 1801.

That same year he was made up to vice-admiral and was sent to the Baltic to attack the Danish navy, which had joined a number of other Baltic countries in trying to break an English naval blockade. Nelson defeated the Danish fleet in the Battle of Copenhagen, but not until he had disobeyed orders to withdraw. Holding his telescope to his sightless right eye, he announced, 'I have only one eye. I have a right to be blind sometimes.' The success of the mission meant that he escaped criticism, and he was given the honour of entering Copenhagen the day after the battle to open negotiations with the Danes. He was made a viscount and put in charge of the Channel fleet, tasked with preventing an invasion of England by Napoleon's armies.

92. Nelson Wanted the Nation to Look After Emma, but after Trafalgar, It Didn't

When Nelson started his affair with Emma in Naples, she was already a well-known figure, having spent time as a minor courtesan, nude-model and hostess back in England. She had had an affair with Charles Greville, but when he tired of her Greville palmed her off on his uncle, William Hamilton. Although Hamilton was very much older than Emma (sixty-one to her twenty-six), she needed a protector, and the couple married in 1791. When she met Nelson after the Battle of the Nile there was a mutual attraction. Nelson later accompanied the Hamiltons back to England, where Nelson's wife Fanny gave her husband an ultimatum: give that woman up or I leave. Nelson apparently replied, 'I love you sincerely but I cannot forget my obligations to Lady Hamilton or speak of her otherwise than with affection and admiration.' Fanny had no choice but to walk away. Nelson went on to buy Merton Place, where he lived for a while with William and Emma, but William Hamilton died in 1803. Within months, Nelson was called to sea again, leaving Portsmouth on board HMS *Victory* and arriving off Toulon in July 1803 to take part in the blockade of the French fleet. After a couple of years fruitlessly chasing after the French under the command of Villeneuve, Nelson returned briefly to England and to a final meeting with Emma. When he sailed for Cadiz in 1805 with orders to engage the enemy, he decided to implement a plan which he had already tried, with great success, at the Battle of the Nile and at Copenhagen. Rather than following naval tradition by sailing parallel to the enemy in a single file of ships, he split up into several squadrons, each with orders to cut through the enemy line, thereby causing chaos and forcing the enemy to break rank. Villeneuve had thirty-three ships against Nelson's twenty-seven. During the encounter, which became known to posterity as the Battle of Trafalgar, Nelson was fatally injured, but the victory he earned was decisive and marked a turning point in the Napoleonic Wars. Thereafter, Britain really did rule the waves.

Nelson's body was lashed to the mast of the *Victory*, before being placed in a lead-lined coffin filled with alcohol, to assist in preservation. The coffin was brought back to England, where Nelson's body lay in state for three days in the Painted Hall at Greenwich. On 9 January, a vast funeral procession accompanied the coffin to St Paul's Cathedral, under an escort of 10,000 soldiers. Nelson's remains were finally interred after a service which lasted for four hours; a ceremony to which Emma Hamilton was not invited. Despite a plea in Nelson's lifetime that the country should look after Emma, she was ostracised and the country closed ranks against her. The financial rewards and the honours were all steeped on Nelson's brother and immediate family. Emma died in 1815 in extreme poverty, aged forty-nine.

93. War with France Meant Income Tax and High Inflation

The Napoleonic Wars proved to be an expense that imposed heavy burdens on the British – and indeed on the French. By the time hostilities ended it is estimated that the war had cost Britain over £830 million. Much of it was covered by the national debt, which spiralled to over £650 million (more than double the Gross Domestic Product) by 1814. The Exchequer tried different ways of raising money by taxation in a vain attempt to keep borrowing down.

For a number of years Britain concentrated the war effort on developing the Royal Navy so that it could blockade the French ships in their ports. This effectively neutralised their navy. Significant numbers of British ground troops were not involved until fairly late in the conflict, but Britain instead subsidised her allies by contributing substantial sums to maintain their forces against the French. What became known colloquially as the 'Golden Cavalry of St George' (after the figure of St George on the reverse of the gold guinea coin used to finance the subsidies) ran into tens of millions of pounds. Hence, in 1793, Britain started to pay Austria a subsidy of £1.5 million each year. In 1803, the Anglo-Russian Agreement obliged the British to pay a similar amount for every 100,000 Russian soldiers involved in the war. At its 1813 peak, some 450,000 soldiers in the Austrian and Russian armies were being financed by Britain, and the following year saw nearly £10 million being paid out in subsidies – a significant proportion of the entire national budget. That was, of course, over and above the cost of maintaining our own army and navy. Having a large army, provisioning it, transporting and arming it and supporting it with a large naval presence forced the Exchequer to look at new ways of raising taxation.

Initially, the government of William Pitt the Younger had tried to fund the war by raising existing taxes on luxury wares. The Seven Years War had already shown that money could be raised by increasing land taxes, and by taxing luxury products such as playing cards. The rate of duty payable on newspapers, imposed under the 1712 Stamp Act, was increased in 1797. A new tax on wig powder was introduced in 1795 to raise revenue, but in fact failed totally and instead wiped out the fashion for wigs almost overnight. Taxes on visible signs of wealth, such as housing, the employment of servants, carriages and so on was increased year by year, but failed to raise the money needed to pay for the fighting. Higher taxes on tea, sugar, beer, salt and soap came in, as well as higher duties on cotton, silk, leather and paper. It reached the stage when it was said that if a thing moved, it was taxed.

In 1800 the government introduced the hugely unpopular Income Tax. Within fifteen years this 'temporary' tax was raising nearly £15 million annually, roughly 22 per cent of the national budget.

94. Napoleonic War Medals Were Awarded Rather Late

On 15 January 1815, in fields near the village of Waterloo, some 15 kilometres south of Brussels, two great armies clashed. It marked the culmination of over twenty years of war between France and Britain, with just a short break when the Treaty of Amiens suspended hostilities in 1802. For Napoleon, even being there was an astonishing achievement. Three years earlier he had led his army of nearly 700,000 men in the invasion of Russia. A series of disasters, coupled with the 'scorched earth' policy adopted by the Russians as they retreated deep into Russian territory, had left Napoleon with supply lines that were severely overstretched. He won a bloody victory at Borodino, but with losses of tens of thousands of men. He succeeded in taking Moscow, only to discover that much of it had been razed to the ground, and instead of negotiating surrender terms the Russians had simply abandoned their capital. Napoleon left the city, his troops exhausted, starving and without any winter clothing. A long retreat followed, during which time the Cossacks harassed the demoralised army, its spirit broken and suffering from hypothermia and starvation. After the appalling rigours of the Russian winter in 1812, only 27,000 soldiers returned.

The Grande Armée had lost its invincibility, and both the Prussians and Austrians abandoned their coalition with France. In Spain, Wellesley's troops, who were helping the guerrillas in the Peninsula War, made dramatic advances in 1812, winning victories at Badajoz, Salamanca and Vitoria, and forcing the French forces out of the Iberian Peninsula. However,

Napoleon had been able to rebuild his main army, recalling over 250,000 war veterans. By 1814 the forces under his direct control numbered some 250,000, and he issued orders to raise a further 900,000 troops, but this was never realistically likely to be attained. In practice, Napoleon chose to advance towards Brussels to meet the Allied Coalition with his elite Armée du Nord, consisting of over 100,000 troops. At the Battle of Waterloo, the Allied Coalition drove the French from the field, winning a decisive victory for the Duke of Wellington, in charge of a large, multinational force, and for the Prussian army under General Blücher. In victory, the Allies exiled Napoleon to the remote island of Saint Helena in the South Atlantic. He died there in June 1821. By that time the Congress of Vienna had sought to impose a balance of power between the various European states by redrawing the entire map of Europe.

For the first time ever, the British government decided to issue a medal to every soldier involved in the three main battles of 1815 (Ligny, Quatre Bras and Waterloo). The medals did not prove popular with the tens of thousands of other British troops who had fought the French over the previous twenty years. They had to wait until 1847, with the issue of the Military General Service Medal, by which time many of their numbers had died.

95. Gas Lighting Enabled Factory Staff to Work Shifts

In 1777, a twenty-three-year-old set out from Ayrshire on foot, to walk the 300 miles to Birmingham to see his hero, James Watt. He was William Murdoch (sometimes the spelling was Murdock). He was keen on engineering and wanted to get a job. Matthew Boulton saw his potential and took him on immediately. In time, he became works manager at the Boulton and Watt factory, and one of his jobs was to travel down to Cornwall to supervise the installation of the company's steam engines. He had been working in the local tin mines near Redruth in 1792, when he started an experiment by burning coal dust in a pipe. Light came out of the other end of the pipe – Murdoch had discovered coal gas. This new form of light was to change the way people lived and worked. In that year he became the first person to illuminate his house with gaslight. From there, he took his invention to the Boulton factory at Soho, in Birmingham, installing factory lights in 1786. This revolutionised factory working conditions. Suddenly, it meant workers could continue to operate their machinery even in the winter darkness of a late afternoon. It enabled factory owners to introduce longer shifts and then night work.

Murdoch went on to make a variety of other inventions, including the pneumatic tube message system still in use in some offices and supermarkets. He worked on the early paddle steamers, came up with a cheap form of isinglass (used as a fining in beer production) and made improvements to the steam engine, including a system for obtaining rotary motion, which Watt was happy to claim as being his own invention. However, it is for gaslighting that he is best remembered. In 1802, the Soho factory lit the newfangled gaslight in an outside display, much to the astonishment of the local residents. The light was somewhat primitive – the gas mantle would not be invented for another 100 years – but improvements came thick and fast.

In particular, a German inventor called Frederick Albert Winsor helped pioneer the development and patented the first gas lamp in 1804. In the same year, Winsor demonstrated the gaslight as a way of lighting the stage at London's Lyceum Theatre. A short time afterwards, on 28 January 1807, he amazed the good people of Pall Mall in London by igniting the world's first gaslit street lamp. It was far more effective than earlier oil lamps or candles. The lamps also proved to be far cheaper to operate, with running costs 75 per cent less than available alternatives. Across the whole country the gas lighting industry took off, and within a few years most large towns were lit by gas, partly because of the cost benefits and partly because the light emitted by the lamps was far superior to other alternatives. Introduced into the workplace and private homes, the new lighting facilitated a boom in literacy.

96. You Couldn't Have Had an Industrial Revolution Without Mr Maudslay's Nuts and Bolts to Hold It Together

Few people remember Henry Maudslay, yet he was a brilliant engineer who made the Industrial Revolution possible. His achievements were staggering. Imagine an earlier scene, where a man sits at a workbench, file in hand, adjusting an individual nut to fit a bolt. When finished, he starts on a separate pair – they are not interchangeable. Fast forward to one of Maudslay's factories, and a machine lathe is churning out thousands of identical, interchangeable nuts and bolts. Maudslay brought precision, standardisation, mass production and accuracy – he even invented a micrometer screw to measure with an accuracy of up to a ten-thousandth of an inch. He was one of the first to introduce an assembly line to manufacturing. His work on the manufacture of industrial lathes, with a three-part combination of lead screw, slide rest and change gears, was a huge advance in machine-tool manufacture.

He was born in Woolwich in 1771. His father died when he was nine years old and times must have been hard. As a twelve-year-old he went to work in the docks as a 'powder monkey', loading cartridges. He moved on to training in a smithy, working with iron, and quickly made his name as a brilliant innovator and a skilled technician. He was commissioned by Bramah (mentioned earlier) to be the person who actually engineered and produced the lock that Bramah had designed, and which proved to be almost impossible to pick. He helped Bramah make the first effective hydraulic press, but after working for Bramah for eight years, and having been made up to foreman, he asked for a pay rise. Bramah refused. He apparently felt that 30s a week was quite adequate, even for a man with extraordinary talents, and so Maudslay left Bramah's employment and set up on his own. It was then that his influence on his apprentices became his biggest legacy. His factory became a centre of excellence to which all aspiring engineers sought admission. If you were a Maudslay man you were marked for the top! He inspired and motivated them, drumming in the maxims by which he worked. In particular, he encouraged clear planning and a dedication to simplifying the manufacturing process.

Later, the business of Maudslay, Sons & Field was based in Lambeth and specialised in the production of marine engines for the Navy. In 1823 the Navy commissioned their first ever steam-powered engines for HMS *Lightning*, using an engine supplied from the Lambeth works. Within thirty years more than 200 vessels were using Maudslay, Sons & Field engines, including the mighty, 750-horsepower engines commissioned for Brunel's SS *Great Western*. Maudslay's factory also manufactured the tunnelling shield designed by Marc Isambard Brunel (mentioned earlier) and produced the gigantic pumps needed to keep the water out during the construction of the Rotherhithe Tunnel. He died in 1831 at the age of fifty-nine.

97. The Queen Was Barred at Bayonet Point from Entering the Abbey

The queen in question was Caroline of Brunswick, the wife of George IV, and the occasion was his coronation in 1821. Married in 1795, the couple had separated the following year. The prince loathed his wife, and carried on his philandering ways with a succession of mistresses. Caroline, meanwhile, behaved somewhat indiscreetly with a number of gentleman admirers. This got to the stage where the prince accused her of having an illegitimate child, a claim which was unsubstantiated, despite a Parliamentary Commission of Enquiry. The public in general sided with Caroline, feeling that she had been most unfairly treated by a man who was regarded with increasing disgust. His womanising, hypocrisy and above all his extravagant spending of public money, made his wife seem like a paragon of beauty and virtue in comparison.

In 1814, Caroline left the country and moved around Europe, leaving scandal in her wake, not least because of her relationship with an Italian commoner called Bartolomeo Pergami. The press, and in particular the caricaturists, had a field day, showing Caroline as a short, dumpy woman carrying on with a tall, bearded Italian. They certainly made an odd-looking couple. The prince wanted a divorce, but realised that any accusation of adultery against Caroline would inevitably lead to much adverse publicity linked to his own errant behaviour. 'Pot' and 'kettle' came to mind. The prince persuaded Parliament to introduce a Pains and Penalties Bill, aimed at enabling Parliament to declare the marriage annulled without the need for a further court of law. The public were outraged and felt that Caroline was being treated most unfairly, and the bill was withdrawn. Her cause became linked to civil unrest, and to radical opposition to a much-despised Prince Regent. Various riots and disturbances took place, and on one occasion troops mutinied.

When her husband acceded to the Crown upon the death of George III, Caroline returned to Britain, intent on fulfilling her role as queen consort. The king informed her that she would not be allowed to attend the coronation at Westminster Abbey, but Caroline was adamant that she had a right to be present and tried to force entry into the abbey. Finding the way barred, she went to another entrance, but found this was also barred to her. Troops were called, and at the point of a bayonet Caroline and her entourage were forced to withdraw. The date was 19 July 1821.

The next day Caroline fell ill: she was convinced that she had been poisoned. Within three weeks she was dead, leaving many unanswered questions as to the cause of death. She was fifty-three, and may well have had cancer of the stomach. Her body was taken through London to the port of Harwich, and from there was conveyed to her native Brunswick. Her tomb bears the inscription, 'Here lies Caroline, the Injured Queen of England.'

98. Only the Rich Got Divorced

In Georgian England, only the rich could afford to divorce. Everyone else either accepted the situation, or simply disregarded convention and moved in with their new partner with no prospect of remarrying. There were, in fact, only two ways of ending a marriage (other than by death). The first was to apply to the ecclesiastical Court of Arches for an annulment, involving an arcane process that could take years and cost a fortune in legal fees. The other method was to introduce a Private Members Bill into Parliament and sit back while MPs debated the lurid and often sordid details of the marriage. This meant that divorce was generally only available to men and to wealthy ones at that. A woman would have to prove that her husband was guilty of something spectacularly wicked, such as incest, bigamy or what was quaintly called 'unnatural vice'. A man merely had to prove that his wife was unfaithful, even if only on one occasion.

The number of divorce cases was incredibly small. Between the reign of Henry VIII and the end of the Georgian era there were just over 300 divorces in total, of which four were at the request of women. Instead of divorce, couples would bring proceedings in what was termed 'criminal conversation', or crim. con. for short. It was finally abolished in 1857. It involved an 'action in tort', conducted at the Court of the King's Bench at Westminster Hall, brought by a husband for compensation for breach of fidelity with his wife. A cuckolded husband could bring a suit demanding astronomical damages against a person debauching his wife. One notorious case in crim. con. was brought by the aristocratic rake Richard Grosvenor, against the king's brother the Duke of Cumberland. It gripped the nation in 1769, because it involved the royal family, and brought to light previously unknown details: what time the royals got up in the morning, what their breakfast arrangements were, when they went to their clubs and so on. It was the first time that such tittle-tattle had entered the public arena and arguably fuelled an appetite which has never diminished to this day. The errant Duke of Cumberland had to cough up £20,000. Grosvenor divorced his wife.

The actual evidence of the adulterous act was usually presented in the form of statements made by witnesses, usually servants. Their testimony was often circumstantial, with much reference to squeaking bedsprings, crumpled sheets and figures departing from bedrooms in the early hours of the morning. The public lapped up the trial reports, and books based on crim. con. cases often gave titillating, voyeuristic insights into the lives of the rich and famous.

Having obtained an award of damages, the cuckolded husband could then decide whether to get a formal separation, or even a divorce. Almost invariably he would be given custody of any children of the marriage, even to the point of the mother being barred from ever seeing them again.

99. Dr Buchan's Work Meant That Anyone Could Recognise a Buboe

Dr Buchan wrote a book entitled *Domestic Medicine*. He was a remarkable man for his time, and his book was an astonishing success, being reprinted over twenty-two times and being hugely influential, both in Britain and in the United States. His masterpiece was more than just the eighteenth century equivalent of the *Readers Digest Book of Home Medicine* – it was a groundbreaker in many ways. The expanded title of the work gives a clue to its target market: *Domestic Medicine: or, The Family Physician: being an attempt to render the medical art more generally useful, by showing people what is in their own power, both with respect to the prevention and cure of diseases.*

William Buchan had been born in Scotland in 1729, and he graduated in medicine from Edinburgh University. After a spell in Sheffield, he returned to Edinburgh in 1766, and spent several years in one of the poorest areas in the country, where he was confronted with ignorance about basic hygiene and cleanliness. He could see that this was causing pain, suffering and premature death. Indeed, he was so upset at seeing that half of all children were dying before their teens, largely because of unhygienic conditions, that he determined to end the mystique that went with the job of being a doctor. As Buchan himself said, 'No part of Medicine is of more general importance than that which relates to the nursing and management of children.'

This was groundbreaking stuff: until then, most treatises were a mixture of witchcraft and mumbo-jumbo. Rather like the Magic Circle trying to guard the secrets of the magician's trade, the medical profession frowned on such openness. But in 1769 Buchan published the first edition of his *Domestic Medicine* and it became a runaway success with the public. The book originally cost 6s, and the nineteen editions published in his lifetime sold 80,000 copies. The work was translated into many European languages, including Russian, French and Spanish.

We may find the advice somewhat rudimentary, but Buchan was working at a time when washing was a rare occurrence. He wanted the public to embrace hygiene as a form of self-help. As well as this, he called for the provision of pure water supplies, publicly cleaned streets and advocated the benefits of fresh air. Exercise and a good diet were also a part of his campaign. At the time, these ideas were nothing short of revolutionary.

Did the book's success make him rich? Apparently not, since he supposedly sold the copyright to his publisher for £700, only to see the publisher recoup as much every single year from sales. Buchan died in 1805 and was buried in Westminster Abbey. Intriguingly, three years later, when the mutineers from the *Bounty* were discovered on Pitcairn Island, it was found that they had kept a copy of Buchan's book with them, wrapped in sail cloth.

Oh, and buboes? They were swellings of the lymph nodes.

100. We Nearly Had Queen Charlotte and Not Queen Victoria

When the Prince of Wales married Caroline of Brunswick in April 1795, it is fair to say that what they had in common was a mutual hatred for each other. The prince only agreed to the marriage in order to get his hands on a greater allowance from Parliament. He was so drunk on his wedding night, to the point of being insensible, that he fell asleep in the hearth. At some point he must have consummated the marriage, because in January 1796, nine months after the wedding, Caroline gave birth to a daughter, Princess Charlotte Augusta of Wales.

She was the only legitimate grandchild of George III, and as such was next in line to the throne after her father, who went on to become Prince Regent and, eventually, George IV. She was brought up by governesses and banned from seeing her mother, who, to all intents and purposes, was banished to Europe. As an impetuous teenager she angered her father, who consigned her to isolation and imposed strict controls on her friendships. She grew into a beautiful, passionate young lady, and one who was not always ready to show royal decorum. After initially agreeing to a marraige with Prince William VI of Orange, she broke off the engagement in spite of her father's insistence that she marry. Instead, she fell for the charms of a succession of impoverished noblemen and princes. Here was a woman determined to marry for love, not money, whatever her father said. Eventually, she married the somewhat impecunious Prince Leopold of Saxe-Coburg-Saalfeld (later to become King of the Belgians). They made a golden couple, the public adoring her for her style, her fashion sense and for being so different to her much-despised father. Tens of thousands turned out to watch as the couple got married at Carlton House. Parliament voted Leopold an income of £50,000 per year and paid for the purchase of their new home at Claremont House.

The princess became pregnant almost immediately, but suffered an early miscarriage. She quickly became pregnant again. Aged twenty-one, she went into labour in November 1817, but the baby, a boy, was stillborn. Tragically, the young mother died of complications the following day. The whole country went into deep mourning, with shops closing for an entire fortnight. The Prince Regent was devastated at the loss of his only legitimate heir, while poor Leopold found himself without either a wife or a child in the space of just twenty-four hours. Much criticism was directed at Sir Richard Croft, the obstetrician in charge of the birth, for his refusal to use forceps. The criticism may have been unfair, but the poor man became suicidal, and shot himself three months later.

Had she lived, Charlotte would have succeeded George IV on his death, as Queen Charlotte. Instead, the crown passed to the king's brother, who became William IV, and then on his death to his niece, the young Princess Victoria.